2nd Edition

Insuring to Value:
Meeting a Critical Need

**Peter M. Wells
and the Editors of
Marshall & Swift / Boeckh**

The
National
Underwriter
Company

Table of Contents

Insuring to Value: Meeting a Critical Need

Foreword

Ten years ago when the first edition of *Insuring to Value* was released, the industry was reeling from the aftershocks caused by a series of record-breaking catastrophes: the Oakland Hills fire in 1991, Hurricane Andrew in 1992, and the Northridge earthquake in 1994. Today we are dealing with the effects of wildfires that raged across Arizona and California in 2003 and a string of hurricanes that hit the Gulf States in 2004 and again in 2005.

The catastrophes of the 1990s formed the book's premise that "total-component" valuation method was the solution to the extensive underinsurance problem revealed by the vast numbers of property claims.

The catastrophes of the first half of this decade remind the industry that, while much has improved, there is still work to be done to reduce incidences of undervaluation and underinsurance. They have also identified more serious issues: the lack of available capital and the reluctance to provide property coverage in areas that are still struggling to rebuild.

What was true in 1995 is true today: undervaluation and underinsurance issues can be addressed and ameliorated by focusing on the principles and methods that were presented in the volume that became recognized as the definitive text on insuring to value.

This new text leads carriers through the proven concept of total-component valuations to a broader definition of insuring to value, one that helps carriers identify the true value of each individual risk. More importantly, it is a roadmap that helps carriers understand and implement strategies and techniques such as data archiving, data analytics, and book of business management that their peers have shown will improve underwriting, risk selection, and decisioning for entire portfolios of property business.

Today, with the property industry still dealing with open claims and coverage litigation in the aftermath of Hurricane Katrina, it is more important than ever for carriers to focus on ensuring that their books of business have appropriate valuations. The continued success of the industry is going to depend on their diligence in upgrading analytical techniques and monitoring their books of business.

Dennis Chookaszian

Retired Chairman and Chief Executive Officer, CNA Insurance Companies

Foreword

Every now and then, perhaps once in a generation, a book comes along that rips open the fabric of an industry's conventional thought. New ideas spill across the business. Eyes, once firmly shut to the future, are opened wide. Innovation flourishes. It is a breathtaking time, and rewarding in many ways to the book's author. It is an event of immeasurable importance.

The publication of the first edition of *Insuring to Value* was not one of those events. It should have been. It was one of those rare books that could change a business, but it arrived at a time when executives in the homeowners business would hear nothing good about the business, would see nothing good in its prospects, and certainly had nothing good to say. Ears stuffed with cotton, eyes glazed over from losses, the industry was in no mood to consider the book's proposition that creative thinking and innovation could change their fortunes.

"Homeowners," said the chief executive of a major homeowners insurer just after the book was released, "is a structurally bad business in which we simply can't make money."

Ten years later, the revelations found in that volume are no less valuable than they were when first introduced. But today we feel much more confident that insurers are ready to listen. Some, the early adapters of the improved underwriting discipline championed by the first edition, are giddy about the strong profits they have found in homeowners insurance. They now see opportunity and are open to new ideas like those offered here.

Others are in a panic over how to adjust to increased catastrophe losses, solutions for which are partially found in the sophistication advocated in this volume. These companies now see real trouble and are ready to reconsider their business practices in search of safer, more stable, earnings.

It is too soon to say just how much of an impact this book will have on the industry it seeks to help. But we can urge only one course of action to those hoping to find greater success in the property insurance business: read on.

Brian P. Sullivan

Editor of the Property Insurance Report

Acknowledgement

Without the efforts of many people, this book would not have been possible. Numerous experts on staff at MSB contributed building cost research, data analytics, historical data, and other valuable insights into building construction trends, component-based valuation technology, and insuring to value. The National Underwriter Company provided the forum to bring this valuable information to the insurance industry. And lastly, I would like to acknowledge the editors at MSB and especially Marsha Berenson, whose efforts were invaluable in bringing this project to conclusion.

About the Author

PETER M. WELLS

President, MSB

Peter Wells is president of MSB, where he is responsible for strategic business planning, product development, and outsourcing services to the underwriting and claims divisions of property insurance carriers.

Prior to joining MSB, Peter served in various management capacities at Software Shop Systems, McGraw-Hill Information Systems, DRI, ACORD, and AMICA Mutual Insurance Company. He is a published author of numerous articles, industry standards, and best practices texts, including the first edition of *Insuring to Value*. He speaks regularly at various insurance conferences and forums. Peter is a graduate of Boston University.

Introduction

In 1996 when MSB, then Marshall & Swift, published the first edition of *Insuring to Value* in collaboration with The National Underwriter Company, the book looked at important construction trends affecting homeowners insurance in North America that had evolved since the Reagan presidency and proposed a change in the way homeowners insurance was written and maintained. Often countercultural in its argument, *Insuring to Value* was a position paper to insurance professionals. The book alerted the property industry that new designs in home construction and the emergence of a remodeling phenomenon as a supplement to new home development were causing a fundamental shift in the manner in which companies would need to value risks. This shift was vitally important to the industry because the risk valuation process, a function the industry had embraced since the origin of the homeowners policy, left unattended, had already led to undervalued and unprofitable property business.

MSB, as a partner in the home insurance market, was keenly aware of the under valuation problem as well as the fact that property writers were regularly experiencing triple-digit operating ratios and were too often unable to maintain profitability. Profitable books of homeowners business in 1996 were the exception, and, in many instances, companies would even fail. Proof that large problems lay underneath a seemingly calm surface was revealed in the outcome of the fires, earthquakes, and storms of the late 1980s and early 1990s. MSB, arguing that the under valuation problem needed to be fully explored and corrected, took the lead in researching the problem, thereafter introducing its findings and recommendations through the medium of the first version of *Insuring to Value*.

Of importance to the research performed was a study of the history of how property writers worked with building cost providers Marshall & Swift and E.H. Boeckh after World War II. This included information on how to develop a home protection and pricing strategy around the new homeowners insurance policy through consideration of the replacement cost that might be incurred if a major loss resulting from an insured peril were to occur. The formula

Replacement Cost x Rate = Premium

was conceived as a central algorithm in the insuring process. Replacement cost, in an era before automation and characterized by very similar residential construction, could be calculated using simple square-foot guides, which were generally printed brochures containing building costs per square foot. The majority of residential construction coming into the marketplace was new tract housing, set up uniformly in homogeneous markets primarily around larger cities. The amount of insurance coverage was in most instances ultimately determined by insurance agents equipped with these simple, easy-to-handle guides as the means of assessing insurable value or replacement cost. Because homes had fundamental similarities, models could be created that approximated the cost to replace various styles of homes taking into account that what was in the model was likely to be in the properties insured; it was simply a matter of fitting the property to the appropriate model in the brochure. Data was delivered quarterly by Marshall & Swift and E.H. Boeckh to their respective clients, helping to keep the industry up-to-date on inflationary trends affecting construction in various local economies.

As we learned after the natural disasters in the early 1990s and presented in the first edition of *Insuring to Value*, upturns in the economy after 1982 led to dramatic changes in complexity to residential construction that would ultimately unravel the efficacy of earlier square-foot brochures. Homes simply stopped being similar and were also increasingly affected by remodeling. The impact of this when concentrations of losses occurred was the fact that property business could no longer be addressed in the same old ways. New valuation initiatives needed to emerge, which effectively became the province of Marshall & Swift and others to research and develop.

The resulting discussion centered on the invention of what we now call "total-component" estimating. Through extensive research on what was hurting property writers, as well as new techniques in database automation, Marshall & Swift recommended the industry reduce its dependence on generic square-foot methods and adopt a new valuation approach. The new approach would work the way contractors did, mixing and matching components of construction through use of modern estimating technology to assemble each unique home based on its component parts. Aligning homes to preconceived models was a process that was failing by 1996. Instead, pricing each home uniquely from the ground up based on its component parts was finally a reality. That insurance companies could begin to utilize this program in virtually any emerging automation platform, with the software actually doing the estimating for the user, was a breakthrough, but one that companies felt they needed to fully understand in order to adopt. Just such an explanation was put forth in the original *Insuring to Value,* with investigative insights that helped make the case.

The emerging affluence that began in the 1980s with the Reagan era led to a fundamental shift in the housing market, wherein home builders were able to provide bigger and more complex structures across the nation to home buyers eager for more upscale properties.

While the construction market had changed during the 1980s, the insurance industry's approach to reconstruction valuation had not. As discussed previously, most carriers still used square footage-based replacement cost estimating tools even at the time that *Insuring to Value* was written. The technology that was developed in the 1990s allowed carriers to effectively capture and use property characteristics data at a granular level to provide risk-specific valuation estimates, especially when dealing with the increasing numbers of homes that were larger or contained mixed construction. Important to Marshall & Swift in particular was the effect its market research had on justifying how better insurable values could be calculated with a more component-oriented approach to insurance-to-value programs. The impact was so dramatic, especially for insurers finding and correcting homeowners coverage that was unreliable, that Marshall & Swift virtually stopped working with the legacy approach to focus its attention on modern total-component estimating. Convincing the industry of the validity of this change has been a ten-year process, but today, as we look back, the majority of property writers are now advocates of the programs and processes outlined a decade ago.

With the help of total-component (also known as component-based) estimating, many levels of improvement occurred not only in operating ratios, but, ultimately, in the competitive advantage property writers experienced in the markets they served. Some companies began major reviews of their books of homeowners business to collect new information about the homes they insured as well as to determine the extent of undervalued properties and the amount of exposure faced. They also sought to upgrade coverage for policyholders, and, at the same time, make premiums commensurate with risk. Others facing financial problems in property business learned that by updating books of business to the modern component approach they were able to stabilize their business while recovering millions of dollars in lost revenues. Still others began to consider ways to archive the vast amount of data consisting of interior and exterior characteristics of homes common to the total component process. This data not only helped them work closer with policyholders year after year but also facilitated detailed analytics that benchmarked their competitive position to others in local markets. And, as a whole, the industry began to realize the benefit of this modern, more exact method of valuing individual properties, which was needed in order to achieve and maintain true insurance to value.

In addition to presenting a more exact way to calculate valuations, component estimating leveraged technology to develop those valuations. This technology included a number of complementary systems. It included lightweight and increasingly ubiquitous Windows™-based applications that would run valuation software, and which insurers could deploy and use more easily than legacy mainframe systems. It included geocoding tools to identify risks with accuracy that enabled inclusion of the specific impact of localized building codes, labor and material rates, overhead and profit, and other market conditions in the replacement cost estimate instead of using generic multipliers and factors. And, ultimately, it included Web-based systems to provide better access to and utilization of cost and component information. With the advent of Windows™, networks, the World Wide Web, and the Internet, the adoption of simple-to-learn-and-use component-based estimating jumped forward dramatically, leaving the era of paper cost guides far behind.

Total component estimating required new thinking and new procedures, including the collection of component-level, risk-specific information at a depth of detail to which companies and agents were not accustomed. Valuation software also lent itself to deployment on a desk-level basis via flexible yet powerful personal computer and network technology platforms, which represented a change for insurers and staff accustomed to mainframes, "dumb" terminals that could only be used to input and display data, and hard-copy building valuation manuals. Therefore, despite the inherent advantages of component-based estimating over the square-foot method, the new method took several years to become widely accepted.

The year 2001 was a benchmark for component-based estimating, when the merger of the E. H. Boeckh and Marshall & Swift to form Marshall & Swift / Boeckh, or MSB marked the beginning of a rapid expansion in the adoption of the approach. Both companies had developed component-based valuation technology independently and believed the market needed it. With the merger of these two leading companies, the movement toward component-based estimating gained even greater momentum

MSB also began providing a broad-based book-of-business updating process called telephone estimating, which combined a detailed property survey with a total-component reconstruction estimate. Although this service was designed to benefit insurers, an added benefit for the industry was that, through data analysis, MSB discovered that a majority of insured homes across the nation was undervalued, the extent of which will be detailed in later chapters in this book. This disturbing fact further solidified the need for an improved valuation methodology in the industry as well as better book-of-business management as a general practice. As of the close of 2005, MSB had helped carriers in their book management by updating more than fifty books of business, which encompassed nearly eight million policy records and also helped to further advance the concept of component-based estimating.

Today, carriers that represent nearly 90 percent of North American property writers are using component-based formulas in their insurance-to-value initiatives. That this change was in fact the right move for the industry has been clearly demonstrated in recent years. For instance, MSB has monitored the underinsurance problem in the market by analyzing archived data from both book-of-business updates and closed claim files. As is detailed in later chapters, this analysis shows that there has been a reduction in both the number of underinsured properties and the overall percentage of underinsurance in the industry, which, by 2005, has ultimately led to a 50 percent reduction in lost premium due to inadequate property valuation.

In addition to taking a giant step forward by adopting component-based estimating in the insuring-to-value process, many carriers have also adopted the same methods and technologies for their claims estimating. In fact, the efficacy of component-based estimating has been clearly demonstrated in total-loss claims. With astounding accuracy, insurance companies have paid amounts for those total losses equal to the replacement costs calculated for properties and, therefore, the limits of insurance carried.

What the industry must do in its continued efforts to reduce underinsurance as well as to deliver the greatest insurance benefit to the public is to further refine its understanding of insuring to value. Calculating accurate reconstruction costs for properties is only the beginning of achieving and maintaining accurate insurable values. The ITV concept should also incorporate a full site evaluation that includes salient on-site and proximate hazard information that will help assess both the desirability of the risk and likelihood of loss. It should include updating coverage limits annually through use of component level home characteristics data that is reviewed jointly with policyholders and agents at time of renewal with resultant recalculations of coverage amounts instead of more general indexing. And, it should include combining claims and underwriting data to begin developing new competitive strategies based upon risk desirability measurements found at each insured location based on each home's characteristics.

Insurance to value is a critical and evolving part of the property insurance business with dimensions that transcend the original concept of building valuations and associated pricing. Just as it is essential to the economy that homeowners insurance be successful, it is likewise important that insurance to value evolve to include all of the various component parts that help qualify and price all facets of property risk found at a given location. In this broader concept of insuring to value, it is even more important to make use of geocoding systems to accurately locate an insured property and to overlay this information with data related to its total exposure for a variety of physical hazards. These hazards include location in or near a fire zone, sink hole, earthquake zone, or storm-surge area, as well as related issues such as whether emergency services can quickly respond to calls at the property location. All of these are as critical to the ultimate adequacy of insurance coverage and insuring to value as is replacement cost. It is also critical to load component-level detail, including on-site and proximate hazards, into a master database in order to assign a series of associated cost factors and loss predictors to the final premium calculated and archive this data for future data mining and business intelligence.

The losses that occurred in the three years ending in 2005 demonstrate to companies that the economic trends they faced in 1989 are cyclical and have similar disastrous effects. However, this time around, the industry was better prepared with better systems and tools and was able to weather the storm. MSB viewed the original edition of *Insuring to Value* as a position statement about the insurance-to-value front of the insurance industry, setting the stage for change that many companies adopted. This edition of *Insuring to Value* is an update for the industry on what has been learned since the first book appeared ten years ago, as well as an outline of where the industry should go over the next decade and beyond.

Like the first book, this new edition offers insights and direction. Our hope is that just as the case for component-based estimating made in that first edition has been proven with experience and time, the options and solutions recommended in this book for better managing books of property business will similarly have profound and positive impacts on the insurance industry. The conclusions derived from the research we will highlight also depict the best strategies for turning around under performing property business, as well as the best fine-tuning activities for well maintained business. It is hoped that all participants in the insuring equation take something important away from reading this edition. The editors at MSB certainly did, because working with their most important resource—their customers—formed the foundation for the observations contained in this book.

As partners to the property insurance industry, MSB is dedicated to future advances and looks forward to working with the industry for the next ten years of progress and success.

Chapter 1

Identifying Homeowners Risk

Background

The advent of homeowners insurance in the early 1950s can be traced to the emergence of a new home buyers' market that developed after World War II, spreading from the eastern part of the United States westward and concentrating around major urban centers. As members of the Armed Forces returned home from WWII (and later Korea), their ability to benefit from education offered by government spending programs like the Servicemen's Readjustment Act (1944), popularly known as the GI Bill, created a new generation of educated civilians who would no longer return to the agrarian society and small towns that typified America before the war. As returning veterans in search of a better life, millions of America's war veterans ultimately settled around major commerce centers like New York City, forging a broadening economic base of educated professionals.

As populations grew, the need for housing to accommodate these millions also increased. Banks and government agencies subsidized housing and provided the economic means to acquire homes closer to the employment environments of workers. With increased lending, the demand for additional financial security in the event of major losses to dwellings encouraged creative property insurers to develop what we now refer to as the Homeowners Insurance Policy. The need for a comprehensive approach to home insurance that would keep pace with home expansion triggered innovation in property insurance circles. The combination of readily available mortgage money, with homeowners insurance as an added means of protection, helped fuel the vast expansion in the homeowners market that occurred.

Simultaneously, new levels of capital encouraged a new breed of home builder to emerge, offering to eager buyers low cost, mass-produced yet desirable housing most often found around urban centers. It was this available, cost-effective housing that more than any other event drew the landscape of America's urban and suburban setting, establishing the foundation for everything from tract housing to today's high-worth communities.

A classic case of what became the bread and butter of the homeowners insurance market at that time is reflected in the residential construction found in communities like Levittown, on Long Island, New York. Begun in the late 1940s, and expanded upon through the next decade, developers of this community used innovative construction techniques to provide interested buyers with a seemingly endless supply of dwelling units at affordable prices, requiring a minimal investment to obtain a mortgage to get started.

The new home developers were corporate entities offering functional living space on basic lots, made affordable by the limited number of simple, yet all-inclusive home designs they created that took advantage of new "stock built" residential construction techniques. Rather than the complex assembly and workmanship of the pre-1930 and 1940 era, these postwar homes were able to be mass-produced, requiring less skill and time to assemble and complete. These revolutionary construction techniques, which were institutionalized through use of modern building codes that still are used today, kept costs and assembly time to a minimum, yet provided an all-inclusive "model" home package that consumers could purchase at a low entry cost. Some of their efficiencies included:

- Machine cut, standard length framing lumber and trim
- Blueboard and plaster (later drywall) replacing 3-coat lath and plaster
- Plywood sheathing
- Mass-produced asphalt shingles
- Standardized, factory-produced concrete block foundation materials
- Slab construction
- Factory-built, easy to install windows with storms
- Standard-sized, factory-built cabinetry
- Hollow core doors
- Metallic-sheathed (BX) and later non-metallic sheathed (NX or Romex®) wiring replacing knob and tube designs

·   More compact, simple to install oil and gas heating units

·   Single-course masonry veneer over framing instead of multi-course masonry

By utilizing these modern, mass-produced materials to construct standard home designs, labor productivity was more predictable, and time per project became systematized.   In large tract developments that emerged, general contractors would allot time to each subsystem to build the homes collectively, rather than individually: for example, all foundations, all framing, all partitions followed by all roofs, etc. Common plans emerged, eliminating excessive overhead for such things as architect's drawings per building. Instead, they were rudimentary. A common set of plans for an entire tract home project would streamline construction, making work simple to follow and complete with less skilled labor. Home builders were thus able to concentrate their purchasing power to build literally square miles of similar housing units; equip them with modern fixtures, appliances, and finishes shipped directly from the manufacturer; and then sell homes at rates more reasonable than ever before.

Mass-produced homes were characterized by relatively square or rectangular footprints with simple shapes and few cut-outs or angles. They had identical concrete block and/or slab foundations, easy to produce and install cabinets, and a general package of basic, precut trim. For simplicity's sake, construction was of three primary categories: frame; less-commonly, frame with masonry veneer; and rarely, solid masonry. Essentially, what drove the home building market was the ability to design and build cookie-cutter style housing that was affordable and that permitted rapid expansion across population centers for average-income individuals. In 1951, a 1,200 square foot total living area (TLA) structure, with basement, basic kitchen and bathroom package, living room, dining space, and three bedrooms was actually built and able to be sold on a small lot for under $20,000 in many economies, inclusive of a 30-year mortgage. Construction took one month or less. Individuals earning as little as $200 per week were able to afford these new homes, the taxes on them, and the basic homeowners insurance to protect them.

As these tract communities multiplied, insurance policies sold quickly because banks began to demand mortgage protection. The insurance industry had never before faced demand of this nature and was under great pressure to respond with sales and underwriting controls for the rapidly emerging mass market. This explosion in tract construction mandated development of insurance processes and procedures that would add speed at the point of sale without sacrificing sound underwriting. These new processes would have to be much less complex and faster to accomplish, and they would have to involve individual risk assessment as well as risk control to finalize insurance policies.

Prior to World War II, risk assessment was performed by limited numbers of loss control professionals and/or underwriters who reviewed what was effectively a limited number of new homes. Underwriters of that era assessed and controlled risk through a time-consuming and complicated process of selecting individual fire-related and liability coverage forms for each home organized on perceived need. In a break-through effort to streamline the insurance sales process for the mass market of the post war era, the insurance industry conceived the homeowners insurance policy: a complete and easier to understand and market policy built around an inclusive number of risk criteria or perils. Because homes were essentially the same across the landscape, the concept of *insurable value* emerged as a prime indicator of coverage need, risk desirability and pricing—a concept that would ultimately be called *Insurance to Value* or *ITV*.

Because so much of emerging residential construction was based on common designs, insurers understood risk similarities existed and reached out to estimating professionals like Marshall & Swift and E.H. Boeckh to confirm their understanding. Working collaboratively with insurers, construction database firms like these helped insurance companies quantify residential construction, identifying that the amount of coverage desired represented a critical ingredient not only in the sales process but, more importantly, in the calculation of homeowners premiums.

Because of home design similarities, it was deemed possible to categorize and value residential property replacement cost, then use this calculation as a prime ingredient in the formula to calculate premiums charged. The formula used for establishing premiums was based upon the cost to replace structures (determined by their correlation to common models of construction known at the time) multiplied by the rate generally applicable for each kind of construction. The calculation was represented by the following formula:

Replacement Cost x Rate = Premium

The ingredients of the rate component evolved over time and were refined by individual insurance providers based on their own claims experience and on aggregated industry experience collected by industry-sponsored rating organizations. As carriers became more sophisticated modelers, rates changed with increased experience and actuarial expertise. Regulators also provided strict oversight to the rating process and controlled the amount of change each carrier could effect, often requiring regulatory input to manage and update rates.

Replacement cost, on the other hand, is based on realities of home construction as it exists in the economy, and thus it is a constant in the formula that is measurable and able to be applied or changed as individual home characteristics are identified. Replacement cost would also become an indicator of risk, because individual carriers' appetites for categories of home values varied, and homes with replacement costs that did not meet their criteria could be isolated.

Developing Replacement Cost Calculation Models

Prior to World War II, establishing the amount of coverage necessary to replace a property if destroyed was possible, but the techniques were complicated and not systematized. Loss control departments relied on large, cumbersome, and very detailed cost manuals; their own professional experience; or limits from policyholders or their contractors. Coverage was provided on a fixed amount basis for individual perils or options.

When coverage limits were questioned, the task of confirming valuation or establishing insurable value fell to loss control engineers or appraisers. These support efforts were time consuming so were performed on an as-needed basis by professionals possessing insight into construction practices and techniques. To help complete surveys, third-party cost data found in information manuals, like Marshall & Swift's *Marshall Valuation Service,* might be used. The lack of automation at the time caused surveys to be time consuming, tedious, and generally not cost effective. Bringing this process forward to the post-war era was unwieldy and totally impractical with respect to the large volume of new tract homes that was emerging. That these homes lacked the complexity of earlier home construction and developed relatively small premiums clearly indicated to insurers that detailed surveys of the type performed in the past were not efficient for determining replacement cost in the new era. Nevertheless, following the premium determination formula, carriers needed to determine insurable replacement cost on every risk written.

Banks also insisted on the availability of insurance protection on every mortgage written before they would be issued. Since homeowners were not prepared to help, the insurance industry began to take an active and scientific role in establishing total replacement cost *before* losses actually occurred.

Mortgage lenders also pressured consumers to acquire sufficient property insurance to protect their loans. This requirement had the effect of creating confusion about the issue of replacement cost for *insurable value purposes.* Because lenders were not familiar with the principles of like kind and quality replacement, or *indemnity* after losses occurred, they focused solely on protection for each individual loan amount. A difference arose leading to the definition of *replacement cost* versus *market value,* which persists even today and has led to more than thirty states enacting regulation mandating replacement cost or indemnity for the insurance policy, not loan value.

Finally, in order for insurance companies to understand the extent of the coverage exposure they could experience when writing new homeowners polices, they needed to develop *a principle of insurable value* that would be applied in the policy contract. In other words, to further streamline the marketing of this vast new product and at the same time capture the overall coverage requirement without complicated field inspection or appraisals, it would be necessary to implement a new principle. The principle was that the homeowners policy would indemnify the insured to the extent that coverage was established when policies were issued. Equally important, it would standardize an efficient medium for using the coverage amount to help calculate premiums charged. From this, *the principle of premium commensurate with risk insured* was systemized and made efficient in the mass-marketing environment carriers faced. Again, because the only tools available to insurance companies to measure insurable value could not meet the pace required by sales volumes, companies looked for new approaches to streamlining homeowners risk evaluation, and alternative methods for establishing reliable home replacement cost were found.

The Evolution of the Risk Evaluation Process

With readily available financing, supported by overall demand and a new base of rapidly expanding home construction, insurance companies seized the opportunity to establish a new and exciting property insurance business. Homeowners insurance emerged as a major source of revenue and growth for property writers. The concentration of similar home construction styles that characterized tract housing presented a perfect opportunity for insurers to mass market the new "homeowners" policy to large numbers of home owners. Sales initiatives were primarily established through the growth of locally established agency operations.

Insurers entering this new space replaced combinations of coverage packages designed specifically for homes with the all inclusive homeowners form, eliminating the need to mix and match multiple polices to cover one risk. Combining essential coverage into a single, all-inclusive program gave insurers, customers and ultimately the sales channel the flexibility and speed necessary to complete large numbers of insurance transactions with minimal effort.

This revolutionary form—the homeowners insurance policy—offered consumers a comprehensive approach to their home insurance needs in a one stop process. It was simpler and more attractive to sell and was easier to rate and bind. Policies provided broad building coverage for a wide range of perils and also included contents, additional living expense, third-party medical expenses and personal liability within the same contract. Simple-to-write endorsements were also available for jewelry, furs, and fine arts. Later developments included coverage for loss to property off premises and even *guaranteed replacement cost*, which agreed to provide complete property restoration if the policyholder maintained a coverage limit of at least 80 percent of the replacement cost value.

The terms of the policy made establishing coverage limits ultimately the responsibility of insureds, but, as we learned, this was not sustainable. Insureds were expected to provide insurable values based on full construction restoration when policies were written and to prove loss when it occurred. Because this was not an easy assessment for the public, homeowners often based their coverage on the estimated sales cost or *market value* of the home; the outstanding mortgage amount for the property; general builders' trends for nearby, newly constructed homes; or input from insurers or their agents. Because this led to imprecise, unscientific, or inconsistent methods for determining coverage limits, alternative strategies that were reliable and consistent were sought.

Because the science of establishing overall building coverage limits reliably in a mass marketing medium was in its infancy, insurance companies wrestled with the role they would play in the process. At the same time, there was a need for the most cost-effective and efficient medium to assist the process, especially because insurers would either benefit or fail from these calculations.

Insurers of the time that were most strategic in their thinking determined that passing the opportunity to value risks to the sales channel at the point of sale made the most sense, especially in light of the large numbers of policies involved. Because most home construction was similar, the outcome was to partner with valuation companies to develop valuation methodologies for the insurance industry that would take into account the new construction of the new tract housing medium with a requirement to merge with mass marketing at the sale level. These methodologies essentially broke from the models set forth for evaluating home construction in the real estate appraisal world; i.e., the anticipated cost of new construction cost for similar properties within adjacent areas, effectively replacing the complex approaches found in earlier manual forms such as the *segregated method* pioneered by Marshall & Swift.

The segregated method is a detailed estimating approach that breaks estimates down to cover major sections and line items of buildings and allows users of the method to identify all the cost components of each section of the structure based on the quantities of materials found. Final estimates are a composite of the costs found in each section of the structure. In most cases, the process requires a rather high degree of construction knowledge, and calculations are made only after determining specific qualities about the property. At the time this method was first introduced, manual calculations were necessary and lengthy field inspections were the norm. This approach was ultimately rejected for valuing tract-type housing because of the need to evaluate a large number of risks in a short period of time before binding coverage.

Actual loss experience was limited at the time because homeowners insurance was so new, so a common set of reference points that were predictable as well as understandable to large numbers of agents and underwriters needed to be established in order to reliably assess claims expense and severity. As a proxy for actual loss experience from settling large numbers of claims, pricing for *new tract home development* was used. This approach, however, omitted specialty costs such as debris removal or loss of economies of scale involved in restoring single homes at unique locations (see Chapter 3 for a more detailed explanation). Automation was also unavailable and computer technology to archive data not yet a reality, so the actual experience of policies written for mass-market housing was not archived or proven. The earliest formulas for establishing home replacement cost values therefore replicated new construction costs, also reducing the calculation to a simple to learn and understand format that relied on a few pieces of data about homes associated with national average level cost tables representative of tract homes of similar construction. This formula later became known as *the square-foot method, b*ecause the square footage of living area of the property was collected along with other basics of similar tract housing.

The square-foot method is fully explored in the next chapter. However, in brief, the square-foot method relies upon a *principle or law of similar structures,* which dictates that home replacement cost is roughly equal to the prevailing square-foot cost for new home construction found anywhere in the nation localized by an adjustment factor. Because residential building codes were only forming at the time, adjustment for location and condition was limited to a wage and material adjustment multiplier applied to the nationalized base cost for the size and style of home. Again, the limited number of home styles of the post-war era made this approach possible. As few as five common styles of homes might appear in any or all local markets across the nation, creating a broad base of similar structures in the overall economy. Age, size, construction (frame, masonry veneer, or masonry), and a quality adjustment for interior finishes were the only other considerations.

Once insurance companies had a valuation process they perceived as easy to learn and use—incorporating an independently developed square-foot cost method with regional multipliers—the model-based square-foot methodology evolved and soon became the standard for underwriting homeowners business. The product derived could fit in a pocket sized guide or pamphlet that was portable and accessible in preautomation days. With this evolution, it became practical for agents and underwriters to actively participate in the valuation process. More evaluations could be completed on a wide range of properties in a shorter period of time, making it possible for companies to continue to expand the mass merchandising of homeowners policies.

As would later be realized, there were substantial differences between construction costs for new tract-ready developments and costs required to restore individual residential properties damaged in insured events. Limited experience and relatively few claims for total losses made it difficult in the beginning to accurately assess all of the variables for which insurance companies would ultimately pay. What the actual experience would be in the many emerging markets around North America was still undetermined. Additionally, the homeowners insurance market, largely sold on a mass-market basis, was growing dramatically and giving insurers a positive cash flow. This, coupled with the lack of loss experience, masked the potential for underinsurance that would later become painfully obvious.

Market Trends: 1960s - 1970s

Growth in adoption of the square foot valuation method was also due to market changes that began in the 1960s and continued into the 1970s. In this era, homeowners insurance continued to expand rapidly with loss experience, in retrospect, still relatively immature. It was an environment that fostered point-of-sale marketing techniques to bind new policies as quickly and efficiently as possible. Market share and revenue growth were optimized. The square-foot method came to be relied on for the determination of insurable values and provided the basis for determining coverage amounts, following the premium determination formula. In this environment, tract homes continued to proliferate and the sales of homeowners policies grew rapidly: By 2003, according to the National Association of Insurance Commissioners (NAIC), the market had grown to over fifty-seven million homeowners policies in the United States (see Appendix 4) and an estimated six million in Canada.

Actuaries also used the generic square foot cost systems as a part of the pricing model for homeowners business. By analyzing construction trends, actuaries indexed cost-related increases in insurable values and, therefore, coverage limits.

While the square-foot method enabled the agent or underwriter to maintain the continuity of the sales process without needing to wait for an appraisal, this method also enabled agents and underwriters to readily modify the resulting valuation if it meant the difference between getting the business or losing it to competition. The simple visible calculations of the square-foot method facilitated this option, which was far too often exercised in the sales process.

Market Trends: 1980s

Beginning in 1982 and continuing through the 1980s, a dramatic shift in the economy greatly affected the home construction market. New-found prosperity of the Reagan area, the advent of the Yuppie generation, and the great increase in two-income families fostered an environment of substantial increases in discretionary spending in which better financed families were able to purchase larger homes with a wide variety of appointments and features. This resulted in a change in the kind of homes consumers demanded, and builders accommodated this change by backing away from the concept of generic tract housing. As the demand for standard tract housing diminished, the norm in home construction migrated to more expensive homes with increased square footage and many more interior and exterior variables of individual design and diversity.

This change in residential construction signaled another dramatic change in the way home replacement costs would be determined as evidence in the amounts claims departments were required to pay. Even though insurance companies were aware of the changes occurring in home construction, by and large they continued to rely on "square-foot" methodologies to determine coverage amounts since the market had acclimated so greatly to this approach.

The changing market created a hidden dichotomy in which larger, more complex homes were being valued with estimating techniques and methodologies conceived for an earlier era. The boom in construction lasted through much of the 1980s and, during that period, more and more homes regularly featured two- and three-car garages, four bedrooms, two or more bathrooms, and large, open, family rooms or recreational areas. Finished basements became more prevalent, and features like central air conditioning, upgraded appliances, and custom cabinetry became common.

The square-foot modeling techniques used to determine costs for dwellings built in the 1960s were now outdated. As more and more upscale, unique homes were being built, it was not uncommon for communities to have similar building designs with greatly differing facades and interior features, even within the same development. The result was a whole new category of residential construction that was typically labeled custom or upscale, with values reaching nearly double or triple those of the earlier tract plans. In hindsight, it was abundantly clear that the newer homes no longer fit into the neatly packaged square-foot models used to represent home values in the 1960s. As a result, insurers learned that they were issuing a large number of homeowners policies with replacement cost valuation requirements well beyond the estimating capabilities of the square-foot methodologies. The potential shortfall in value left a void in the valuation process that is only now being resolved. Competitive pressures in the homeowners marketplace, a trained sales force, the lack of economically feasible alternative valuation systems, and other market dynamics kept most companies from building or adopting alternative building estimation tools.

Another phenomenon, cash flow underwriting, emerged during this period. As carriers began to experience homeowners underwriting losses with greater frequency, they were able to offset these losses by investing the cash generated from premiums. Income from these investments became more and more significant when high interest rates occurred in the environment of the late 1970s and early 1980s, with the prime rate at one point reaching 20 percent. Investment earnings formed the basis of cash flow underwriting. Ultimately, this phenomenon was a disincentive for carriers to come to grips with a growing underinsurance problem that was building in their book of property business.

Market Trends: Late 1980s Shift

Near the close of the 1980s, a recessionary trend decreased new housing starts dramatically. Of the limited number of homes that were built, an increasing percentage included custom homes tailored to the more affluent segment of the market. On the other hand, another emerging new trend was the rapid growth of the home remodeling industry serving those consumers who were unable to trade up, yet who could afford to upgrade, remodel, or expand their existing dwellings. For the first time, the rate of spending on remodeling construction began to surpass that of new home construction. Typically, insurance companies continued to evaluate their risks using square-foot methodologies and, for the most part, attempted to adapt the older valuation methodology to the new construction and remodeling trends.

With fewer new homes being built and more existing homes being remodeled, growth in homeowners policy writing became increasingly difficult. More companies began competing in a limited growth game. Because the square-foot systems were still very much in common use, companies that continued to focus on increasing market share were encouraged to concentrate on securing new business rather than addressing the problem of valuation accuracy.

By 1994, according to the National Association of Home Builders, the remodeling market had grown to $115 billion. Building trends suggested that the insurable value of a given group of homes would increase by an average of 3 percent per year, simply as a result of remodeling activities occurring in the homeowners building stock. This trend was in addition to normal inflationary increases in construction costs. At that time, few carriers had procedures for either identifying or reestablishing current replacement cost limits in the face of these ongoing changes. Instead, they continued to use square-foot methodologies to value structures and simply modified these values by applying to their books a single, broad-based and generic cost factor to portions of books of business. This is one factor contributing to what many insurance companies soon came to see—an understatement of insurable values in 75 percent of the market place by as much as 35 percent from the coverage amounts that should have been in effect.

As fully discussed in Chapter 4, another significant trend that occurred during this period was the rapid move to guaranteed replacement cost policies. For a variety of seemingly sound competitive reasons, these broader policies were sold for virtually no additional premium. The long-term effect this had, however, was to significantly curtail the motivations of homeowners and agents to keep coverage amounts up-to-date.

As homeowners remodeled their properties, they assumed there was little need to inform their agents or carriers of these changes (and have their premiums increased accordingly), because they felt protected under the guaranteed replacement cost umbrella. This was in spite of the fact that guaranteed replacement cost endorsements generally included the provision that the insured agree to insure the home at full value and to report to the insurance company any alterations that increase the home's value by 5 percent or more. All too often, however, insureds neglected to read their policies and, all too often, homes were inadequately insured from the start.

Confidence in guaranteed replacement cost forms became so pervasive that carriers often became the victims of adverse selection in terms of coverage amounts. If a homeowner felt the policy premium might be too high for any reason, he or she would be motivated to shop elsewhere for a policy. Conversely, if the coverage amount was below the home's replacement cost, neither the homeowner nor the agent was economically motivated to rectify the situation because the home was covered by a guaranteed replacement cost policy. As a result, many carriers developed broad bases of business characterized by a disproportionally high percentage of undervalued risks, with no practical method of remedying the situation.

Market Trends: 1990s Dynamics

In the 1990s, a new phenomenon occurred that had not been evident in prior eras. Communities were decimated by natural disasters, which included Hurricanes Andrew, Fran, and Iniki (see Appendix 3); major fires; and earthquakes. Never before had this many disasters affected so many insureds since the homeowners policy was first conceived.

As previously stated, insurers had anticipated their worst-case claims scenario would be limited to the insurable value on a particular policy. However, due to policy provisions, such as guaranteed replacement cost, and regulatory pressure (both of which are explored in more detail in subsequent chapters), insurers often found that settlements far exceeded coverage limits. As a result, the industry experienced a five-year running combined ratio for homeowners business through 1995 that averaged 124.9 percent. This meant that, on average, the industry was paying out $1.25 for every $1.00 they received in premiums. This was in direct contrast to A. M. Best's statement that the industry *should be* operating at a combined ratio of 96 percent or, stated another way, should have operating earnings of $0.04 for each $1.00 of premium. Clearly, catastrophic losses were abnormally high during this period; however, they only amplified the inevitable truth—that the base business was unprofitable.

The first reaction by insurance companies to these adverse financial pressures was to cut costs where possible and downsize accordingly. The second response as a result of these financial pressures was to focus on working "smarter." Many carriers evaluated expert systems to streamline communications, decision-making, and other work efforts. They also considered new and creative approaches to their business, such as outsourcing those tasks that were not within their core competencies and were better done by organizations that specialized in those areas. Similarly, insurers invested more in services and technologies directly involved in their core business that showed promise to result in significant paybacks.

Ultimately, there was not enough room in the cost structure of carriers for these measures to close the profit gap. To restore the industry to a reasonable level of profitability, premium increases would have to be part of the process. However, government regulators forbade wholesale, across-the-board increases in pricing.

With their ability to raise rates restricted by regulatory oversight, insurers began to seriously reevaluate how to address a key area of the insuring equation they could control—how to better value properties. Knowing they had to develop coverage limits more appropriate for the risks they were insuring, yet another revision to the formula used for premium determination was needed:

Replacement (Reconstruction) Cost x Rate = Premium

In this version of the formula, carriers took a renewed look at the settlement experience they faced, concluding replacement cost was not complete if based solely on new construction techniques and further concluding that reconstruction cost, rather than new construction cost, was the overall important ingredient in the estimating process. However, the problem of adequately determining replacement cost consistently on a mass basis continued to be difficult for the industry to solve based on the limited technology dimensions of the current square foot approach.

Government studies following natural disasters of this period also revealed that many insurance companies knew very little about the housing stock they insured and that evaluating risks using square-foot-type cost processes had not given them a true indication of the extent of their exposure. Those that based their pricing on rating entire classes of buildings with common square-foot programs, utilizing index factors to update limits for renewal business, were found to be inadequately protected. Furthermore, information developed by Marshall & Swift and E.H. Boeckh demonstrated the breadth of the diversity of housing characteristics emerging in the United States. These pervasive differences began to underscore the reliability of continuing use of model-driven insurance-to-value systems. (See Appendix 2 for more information on the subject.)

As natural disasters kept occurring, it became clear that unless the industry could properly revalue and update their legacy books of homeowners business and write policies with a more comprehensive valuation approach, failures would occur or less successful companies would be taken over. As a result, the industry began to experiment with structural retrenchment in the valuation process the likes of which had not been known since homeowners insurance was first introduced. At this same time, homeowner insurance writers re-evaluated their business process including modification to policy conditions, deductibles, replacement cost options, and endorsements, introducing alternative business practices that would more adequately address the situations they were facing. Exclusions and coverage lapses began to be enforced, and new loss control mandates were built into policies, especially in geographic areas with high exposure to catastrophic losses. In hurricane and earthquake zones, the policy itself became a loss control mechanism through the use of exclusionary language and other special eligibility requirements. In other cases, alternative insurance available through state-operated Fair Access to Insurance Requirements (FAIR) plans and the use of specific coverage endorsements proliferated. However, a thorough analysis of all these practices suggested that a better way was needed to bring the business back to a sound financial footing.

The insurance industry began to form a consensus that it must reestablish the coverage and premium base for the homes insured, including a more risk-specific approach to valuing and underwriting each property. Out of this consensus a trend emerged in which carriers either embraced new approaches and technologies for estimating replacement costs or faced leaving the market completely. What the industry needed were valuation systems that were more reconstruction cost oriented, addressed the remodeling phenomenon and/or new upscale housing boom, programs more similar to the original segregated methods yet simpler to implement and encompassing more of the characteristics and functionality of the homes insured.

The Current Market

As in the 1990s, financial pressures of the new millennium were bringing about changes in the industry. Many carriers began questioning their traditional ways of doing business. More and more frequently, outside managers have been brought in to take a fresh look at the economics of the insurance business. All seem to agree that homeowners insurance is still a vital enterprise affecting not only the carrier, but also the nation's economic viability and home ownership, as well as regulatory bodies, rating agencies, and reinsurance. After the natural catastrophes of the 1990s and the wildfires and hurricanes of 2003 through 2005, most homeowners in the United States have a much greater appreciation for and interest in their homeowners coverage and the concept of insuring to value.

Chapter 2

Legacy Valuation Methodologies

The history of homeowners' insurance business after World War II, described in the previous chapter, eventually taught property writers that the financial viability of their business is directly linked to establishing accurate, defendable insurable values for each risk insured. From the beginning, the need to develop fast and efficient methods for establishing accurate home replacement costs was recognized, the path to success that followed contained a series of evolutionary steps, and the trail the industry followed toward this goal was to involve this need utilizing the automation technology available at various points in time.

Earliest Methods of Estimating: Segregated Cost

Systematized approaches to estimating residential and commercial building costs independent of actual construction project work evolved during the Depression when valuation companies began publishing typical costs to build key systems for a majority of residential and commercial building types. These companies developed techniques for researching and publishing costs using a large number of sources (including actual building projects) to develop the first independently verified cost data for sale to interested markets, including real estate appraisal, lending, and insurance. As early as 1930, these companies began creating and delivering price sheets, and, as the information grew in depth, compiled manuals of carefully researched data.

In addition to the cost data itself, the Segregated Cost Method was a proprietary process designed by Marshall & Swift to enable users to develop estimates of building cost at a detailed level, incorporating components of construction with separate consideration for major building assemblies and systems. Users would then add these cost components together in a proprietary process to arrive at a reliable building cost. The eventual depth of the database involved required users of this method to possess a significant degree of understanding of construction techniques, as well as the basic differences in quantity, material grade, or workmanship that affect each component of a building. The product became the preferred tool for quantity surveyors, real estate appraisers, insurance adjusters, and loss control engineers.

To facilitate the application of these individualized costs, cost elements were grouped so that all prices related to a similar section of a building, e.g., floor area, could be collected, added together, and applied uniformly to surface areas involved. All wall area costs could be added together and applied to the wall area, all roof costs applied to the roof area, and so on. The simplification of the Segregated Cost Method resulted in the development of the square-foot approach, which became the standard to value buildings in the mass-market environment when homeowners insurance emerged.

Following is a diagram showing how the components are segregated for a single-family residence.

Segregated Cost Method

Figure 2.1

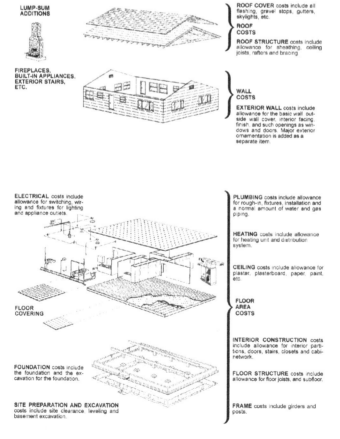

Square-Foot Methodology

Marshall & Swift and E.H. Boeckh became the leading providers of the square-foot methodology to the insurance industry. Each developed a series of modeling techniques that used common features of then-predominant tract housing to establish a base cost value for properties; this value could then be locally adjusted using a series of adjustment factors called multipliers. Square-foot cost systems became available for both dwellings and commercial buildings.

The term "square-foot method" was used due to the fact that a single square-foot measurement for the entire structure replaced the multiple measurements required in the segregated method. Measurements of the outside dimensions determined the number of square feet in each building structure to be valued. The square footage cost of dissimilar structures such as porches or patios would normally be listed separately, because these have a different construction cost per square foot than a home. These separate square-foot cost additions would be added to the cost of the main structure to value the entire building.

Homes that were highly customized, had unique construction characteristics, or were constructed on atypical sites requiring special design (such as hillside construction) would normally require professional assistance for proper valuation.

The square-foot method required a number of steps to determine a valuation. Marshall & Swift developed a seven-step method, which is described in the following discussion.

Step 1: Determine Construction Grade and Quality

Using a single-family dwelling as our example, it was first necessary to select the construction grade and quality that most closely fit the home. Four categories were available: Economy, Standard, Custom, and Luxury. The definitions follow:

Economy

Built from stock plans to sell at low costs, these are usually tract-built development homes. They meet minimum building codes, with materials and workmanship following the same basic pattern. Special-use rooms such as dens or recreational areas are uncommon in this category.

Standard

Construction typically comes from standard plans, with rather simple designs. Workmanship and materials are normally average or slightly above average in quality. They meet minimum building codes and may exceed them in certain instances. These houses often have such areas as a dining and/or family room, with some ornamentation and trim. Most U.S. housing stock falls within this category.

Custom

Constructed from special plans or modified standard plans with custom alterations, these homes generally exceed building codes, use good-quality materials and workmanship, and are attractively decorated. Homes with special use areas such as a dining or family room, den, foyer, and pantry almost always fit into this category.

Luxury

These one of a kind, architect-designed homes with custom features exceed building code standards and feature excellent-quality materials and workmanship. Oversized rooms are common. They often include a number of special use areas including libraries, media rooms, and exercise rooms, as well as special or elaborate decoration and trim.

Step 2: Determine Type of Dwelling

The type of home was selected from eight different styles:

Ranch (1 Story)

A residence with one story of living area. The roof structure has a medium slope. The attic space is limited and is not intended for living area.

Cape Cod (1-1/2 Story or 1-3/4 Story)

A residence with two levels of living area, characterized by steep roof slope and dormers that project from the roof with windows on the front, as shown in the illustration. Because of the roof design, the area of the second floor is usually 40 to 60 percent of the ground floor area.

Colonial (2 Story)

A residence with finished living areas on two floors. The areas of both floors are approximately equal. The roof structure has a medium slope. The attic space is limited and is not intended for living area.

Victorian

A residence with 2-1/2 or 3 stories of living area, typical of a common architectural style of the late 19th century.

Town House (Row House)

An attached single-family residence. Each town house unit is one of a group of two or more units joined by common walls. Such units never have units above or below, always have individual exterior walls, and never have more than two walls common with adjacent units. An end unit is at the end of a row, with only one other unit adjacent to it. A center unit is inside a row, with other units on either side.

Contemporary

A residence designed from combinations of square and rectangular geometric patterns, blending both interiors and exteriors. Contemporary residences typically contain multiple roof lines, where roofs are flat or nearly flat with a slight pitch (shed roof). Exteriors are often plain with little or no ornate trim. The designs of these residences are more modern and less traditional. They typically have open interiors with many variations on upstairs and downstairs living areas.

Split-level (Tri-level)

A residence that is divided either front or rear or side to side, with three levels of finished living area: lower level, intermediate level, and upper level. The lower level is immediately below the upper level as in a two-story residence. The intermediate level, adjacent to the other levels, is built on a grade approximately one-half story higher than the lower level. Split-level residences have a split roof design.

Bi-level (Raised Ranch, Split Foyer, Split Entry)

A residence with two levels of living area, with a lower level being partially unfinished and normally partially below grade (and with no basement below it). The entrance is a split-foyer entrance.

Step 3: Calculate the Ground Floor Area

Calculating the ground floor area was next. The calculations were based on the dimensions of the floor at grade level. The dimensions of the basement, garage, and porch were noted but not included in the ground-floor calculation.

Step 4: Select Construction Materials

The next step was to select the kind of construction material used in the home from a list of only three common materials: frame, masonry, and masonry veneer.

Frame

Constructed of wood frame and covered with wood clapboard or a siding material of aluminum, asbestos, stucco, asphalt, or vinyl.

Masonry

Constructed entirely of masonry except for floor joints, subflooring, interior partitions, and roof members. Common exteriors are face brick, common brick, stone, and split block.

Masonry Veneer

Brick or masonry veneer is frequently used on homes of frame construction. In these cases, adjustments must be made to the frame base cost.

Note that at the time when the model-based square-foot valuation method was developed, the majority of homes, and especially tract homes, were very simple in design and were more easily categorized as frame, masonry, or masonry veneer. Today, studies show that 46 percent of homes in the market are mixtures of these exterior wall materials.

Step 5: Calculation of Base Replacement Cost

Once a determination had been made regarding construction grade, home type, ground floor area, and the type of construction material, it was possible to calculate the base replacement cost by using a table similar to Figure 2.2.

This table shows square-foot costs for a 1-story dwelling in four construction grades and a range of sizes.

Figure 2.2

1-story	Economy		Standard		Custom		Luxury	
Use the Following Table for Home Built After 1940 (Square Footage of Ground Floor)								
	Frame	Masonry	Frame	Masonry	Frame	Masonry	Frame	Masonry
800	60.90	68.60	69.40	78.10	87.90	97.90	108.60	120.90
900	57.20	64.50	66.20	73.10	86.70	85.00	107.10	117.30
1000	56.70	63.70	65.40	72.10	85.40	93.50	105.50	115.50
1100	54.80	61.10	61.40	69.00	82.00	89.10	101.30	110.10
1200	53.30	59.50	60.30	66.70	78.50	85.40	97.00	105.50
1300	53.10	58.40	59.80	65.70	78.00	83.90	96.30	103.70
1400	52.40	57.50	59.50	64.90	75.70	81.70	93.60	101.90
1500	51.80	56.20	58.10	63.40	73.30	80.40	90.60	99.30
2000	49.70	54.80	56.20	61.30	68.30	74.70	84.40	92.20
2500	48.10	52.90	53.80	58.10	65.50	70.20	81.00	86.70
3000	46.70	50.60	52.20	56.30	63.50	67.90	78.60	84.00
3500	45.40	49.30	50.70	54.90	61.90	65.80	76.50	81.30

Step 6: Additional Features

Once the base cost had been determined, the costs of specific features the dwelling might have (such as two-car garage, finished attic, fireplaces, etc.) could be added, as shown in Figure 2.3

Additional Features

Sample of a table from which the cost of additional features could be added to or subtracted from the Base Cost.

Figure 2.3

Once that base cost has been determined, the costs of specific features the dwelling might have (such as two-car garage finished attic, fireplaces, etc.) can be added.

Additional Features
(Sample of table from which the cost of these features can be added to or subtracted from the Base Cost).

Bath (extra)	Economy	Standard	Custom	Luxury
Half bath	$1,210	$1,350	$1,630	$2,000
Full bath	$2,250	$2,530	$2,870	$3,070

Figure 2.3 (cont"d)

Garage (built-in)	
For garages built into the residence at grade level with normal living space above, deduct:	
One-car	($3,610)
Two-car	($5,180)
Three-car	($6,770)

Garage (attached) add:		
	Frame	**Masonry**
One-car	$8,730	$9,600
Two-car	$11,440	$12,570
Three-car	$14,890	$16,470

Step 7: Application of Location Modifiers

Location modifiers, specific to three-digit ZIP or three-character postal code areas, were also available to help adjust costs at the location of the home.

Figure 2.4

APPLICATION OF LOCATION MODIFIERS	
Location modifiers, specific to ZIP code areas, are also available to help adjust costs in the specific location of dwelling.	
Location Modifiers	
For this ZIP Code First 3 Digits	Use This Modifier
Alabama	
350, 351, 354	0.79
352, 355	0.79
356	0.79
357, 358	0.78
359	0.79
360, 361	0.78
362, 368	0.79
363	0.78
364	0.80
365, 366	0.82
367	0.78
369	0.80

The results of steps one through seven were entered on a form and used to calculate the estimated replacement cost:

Figure 2.5

Form 1 **Estimated Replacement Cost Form** **For Use With The Square Foot Method**

(a) Number of Square Feet of Ground Floor Area
(b) Base Cost
    (1) From Chart $_____
    (2) Computed Base Cost (a x b) $_____

(c) Additional Features
    (1)_____ $_____
    (2)_____ $_____
    (3)_____ $_____
    (4)_____ $_____
    (5)_____ $_____

Total of (b)2 and c $_____

(d) Location Modifier From Chart   x_____
(e) Estimated Replacement Cost   _____

The square-foot method offered ease of use to field personnel, who did not have to be trained in complex construction techniques. Because detailed information was not necessary, this method provided a flexible, fast tool for roughly estimating the replacement cost of homes. It was also preferable to another method used at the time, the room-count or unit-count method, which relied on very little information about the home.

Room-Count or Unit-Count Method

A variation on the square-foot method that came about at the height of the demand for homeowners insurance was the room-count or unit-count method. The unit-count method was used exclusively on residential structures. The guidelines for the use of this method involved counting the total number of construction units and rooms found in a dwelling. A unit was a room of a predefined size (either small or large) or a special feature like brick exterior walls or central air conditioning.

The end product provided to the insurance user was a collection of generic model costs that, when added together, would approximate a home's replacement cost. Most of the costs were similar and reflected the law of similar structures discussed previously.

Following is an illustration of a five-step unit count valuation process.

Step 1: Unit Count

The first step was to count the total number of construction "units" found in the home. Each full unit was counted as "1" and each half unit, as "1/2." Figures 2.7 and 2.8 list an array of possible full and half construction units.

Figure 2.6

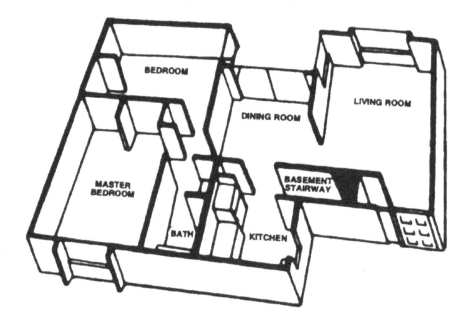

This sample home has a finished basement and finished attic. According to the tables shown in Figures 2.7 and 2.8, the home has ten units—eight are on the first floor, one is on the second floor (finished attic), and the last one is a finished basement.

Step 2: Construction Class

Construction class (grade and quality) of the home as economy, standard, custom, or luxury was determined as described previously in this chapter.

Figure 2.7

List of Full Construction Units (150 Sq. Ft. and Over)
Kitchen
Dining Room
Living Room
Den/Study/Office
Family/Recreation Room
Bedroom(s)
Bathroom(s) (three or more fixtures)
Utility/Laundry/Sewing Room(s)
Finished Basement (omit if counted as family/rec room)
Attached Two-Car Garage
Finished Attic
Partially Finished Attic (count as ½ if not 150 Sq. Ft.)
Partially Finished Basement
Brick/Stone Exterior Walls
Central A/C
Aluminum/Vinyl Siding
Large Wall Fireplace
Enclosed Porch/Breezeway
Clay Tile or Slate Roof
Any Other Unit Not Listed Here

Figure 2.8

List of Half Construction Units (Under 150 Sq. Ft.)
Half Bath
Large Open Porch/Breezeway
Standard Fireplace
Unfinished Basement
Attached One-Car Garage
Built-in Two-Car Garage/Carport
Utility/Laundry/Sewing Rooms
Foyer/Entrance Hall
Dressing Room/Walk-In Closet
Unfinished Attic
Finished Attic
Mudroom (with separate entrance)
Brick/Stone Veneer (Front Wall)
Dinette or Partitioned Breakfast Nook
Any Other Unit Not Listed Here

Step 3: Base Value from Table

As with the square-foot method, an appropriate base value was selected from a table like the one in Figure 2.9

Step 4: Location Modifiers

As with the square-foot method, a location modifier was selected based on three-digit ZIP code or three-character postal code.

Figure 2.9

Base Value for Homes Built after 1940				
Construction Units	Economy	Standard	Custom	Luxury
9	81,800	95,800	116,800	129,200
9.5	85,800	99,800	121,400	134,000
10	87,900	104,000	125,900	139,200
10.5	93,600	108,100	130,300	144,100
11	97,500	112,000	134,900	149,000
11.5	101,300	116,000	139,900	153,900
12	105,100	120,100	144,600	158,800
12.5	108,800	124,100	149,500	163,600

Figure 2.10

Estimated Replacement Cost Form For Use with the Unit Method	
Multiply the base cost (Step 3) by the location modifier (Step 4)	
$_____	(A) Base Cost (Step 3)
X_____	(B) Location Modifier (Step 4)
$_____	(C) Estimated Replacement Cost

Step 5: Final Valuation

The replacement cost was calculated using a form similar to Figure 2.10

Automating the Valuation Process

Room-count and square-foot cost guides printed in pocket-sized booklets were very popular in the 1970s and 1980s, if for no other reason than that there was no easy way to automate this process. Although computer platforms became extremely sophisticated, relatively inexpensive to obtain, and portable, homeowners carriers and their agents continued to print and distribute cost guides, seeming to overlook the empirical evidence that negated the value of this outdated approach.

Automation should have provided the medium to overcome the problems of efficiently and consistently gathering the amount of information needed to properly value homes. In today's world, it is hard to imagine developing reliable replacement cost estimates based on the law of similar structures, especially because similar homes on the same block can and do vary greatly. Nevertheless, too many companies and vendors not only continued to use the printed guides and booklets but also went so far as to automate the square-foot process, thereby prolonging their valuation problems.

The first step to automating correctly is to consider the ultimate goal of both the carrier and the insured—to capture risk-specific information about each insured property, simply and efficiently, and then use this information to develop an accurate home replacement cost for each unique structure. Marshall & Swift and E.H. Boeckh both developed systems that permitted the user to electronically calculate valuations using the square-foot process. Later, both companies took the process a step further by developing component-based estimating systems.

Chapter 3

Total Component Estimating

In the 1980s, both Marshall & Swift and E. H. Boeckh, working independently, made a move toward meeting the needs of the changing housing market by developing component-based valuation methods. Dubbed total-component estimating by Marshall & Swift, these technologies were the precursors of the valuation technologies used today by nearly 90 percent of North America's homeowners insurers.

Today's total-component valuation systems are fully automated. Powerful computer systems process thousands of complex algorithms using enormous amounts of information behind the scenes to accurately evaluate the broad range of components found in North American homes (for more detailed information, refer to Appendices 1 and 2) . The programs also permit users to value a great variety of homes because they deal with the unique features of each property based upon these building blocks that are easy to assemble and reassemble, eliminating the struggle of trying to fit real properties into hypothetical or common models. This advantage is the reason that in most areas, total component estimating was able to quickly replace the square-foot method. Also, with more homes undergoing renovation and remodeling, component methodology allows users to address the constantly changing variable parts of existing housing stock, capture these changes, and adjust the valuation.

A component-based system is an expert system incorporating the methodology of the detailed estimating process that was once performed by the loss control professional or appraiser utilizing construction estimating techniques following in the footprints of the Segregated approach. Because this process is fully automated, it takes very little time to identify—even though the program assembles the component parts of an entire structure using simple descriptions of each property that are commonly available.

Forces Driving Use of Component-based Estimating

Although component-based estimating is today the prevailing valuation method in the property insurance industry, it took a convergence of events to lead the industry to adopt it. In addition to the profitability problems plaguing insurers in the 1980s and 1990s, the evolution of more upscale homes, the complexities of old and new residential construction in similar markets, and a drive toward increased flexibility and effectiveness in the estimating process drove the industry toward a new approach to building valuation.

A number of significant regulatory changes affecting construction further complicated the landscape, suggesting the need for change in the valuation process. First, regulatory mandates that emerged following the natural disasters of the late 1980s led to the introduction of vast numbers of new, complex local building codes that could not be easily included in the design of the square-foot method. Yet they needed to be implemented in the calculation of residential replacement cost.

Next, more concentrated home markets, or local economic cells, were expanding inside earlier identified county level and /or 3-digit ZIP or postal code segments. This growth and spread of home construction markets compartmentalized into a variety of distinct economic arenas with their own construction formulas became a noticeable variable when localizing construction cost data. These are discussed in more detail in Chapter 6. This change had the effect of undermining the validity of earlier square-foot multipliers that relied on the assumption that homes located in broad areas with the same first 3 digits in their ZIP or postal codes were generally uniform, as had been the case prior to the 1980s.

As previously mentioned, dual income families were also emerging that could afford larger homes with more amenities, driving the demand for upgrades and special features as well as competition among builders. Even in tract developments, major differences in home offerings were expected, including custom built kitchen and bath upgrade options, specialty rooms (such as family rooms in addition to living room areas), multi-car attached garages, three or more bedrooms, elaborate decks, finished basements, and specialty glass windows and doors.

Additionally, beginning with the competition for more upscale housing by the so-called Yuppie generation, the *remodeling phenomenon* and the "Home Depot" or home improvement era developed, driven by those families with lower or fixed incomes who found it difficult to trade up to the new level of customized homes being built. This remodeling phenomenon brought about an undercurrent of changing building characteristics both in the marketplace and in insurers' books of business. Remodeling, which often included enhancements to major structural elements of homes, changed the landscape of major portions of the existing home construction market. With all of the reported changes, home replacement cost values were clearly difficult to assign as a simple square foot value; at the same time this mix of construction variables made replacement costs higher.

From a $42 billion market in 1982, this industry evolved into a world-wide phenomenon that later surpassed new home construction. As of first quarter 2006, residential remodeling in the United States was reported to be $215 billion and projected to rise to nearly $240 billion for 2006, according to the National Association of Home Builders. The remodeling trend grew exponentially and its momentum has now slowed, even as demographics have changed.

Today, according to the Joint Centers for Housing Studies at Harvard, over half of all remodeling expenditures and more than 60 percent of all spending for room additions were undertaken by Baby Boomers[1]. The studies also indicate that Generation Xers and immigrants play a large role. As of 2003, the number of Gen X homeowners stood at 12.4 million, with remodeling expenditures by this group estimated at $28 billion. Foreign-born homeowners totaled 6 million, with remodeling expenditures in this group exceeding $10 billion[2].

Just as with new housing, the overall changes occurring in housing stock made it increasingly more difficult for carriers to assume that homes already on the books had standard interior or exterior characteristics that fit the methodology of earlier model-based estimating tools. Homogeneity was no longer the rule, as competitive building options changed from similar to distinct. By the late 1980s, homes no longer fit neatly into model-based valuation programs, because the assumptions for modeling, including the "law of similar structures," could no longer be confirmed if homeowners did not report all of the hidden variables commonly found. Carriers also had a difficult time addressing their changes or fitting them into estimating models.

Finally, computer power was evolving rapidly at the time, suggesting that more robust estimating techniques could be developed without adding more manual complexity to methods of estimating. Effectively, computer advances made a fortuitous appearance at a time when the economic base was undergoing rapid change and valuation methodologies were in need of innovation.

Toward Efficiency and Ease of Use

By the 1980s, home inspections had replaced quantity surveys as a means to help confirm risk desirability and building values for carriers and their agents. When questions arose about coverage adequacy, the industry had traditionally relied on third party vendors to visit homes, gather information, and confirm insurable value using the carrier's approved estimating approach, often the square-foot method for the valuation portion of each assignment.

However, as mentioned earlier, completing site reviews became more difficult because dual-income consumers were often not home. Inspectors were therefore unable to enter homes in order to identify interior features and finishes and evaluate those factors that made houses unique, including costly upgrades, kitchen or bath remodeling, finishes to basements or attics, etc. Inspectors relying on exterior observations only (the original "drive-by" inspections) were also unable to uncover the many possible mixed construction characteristics hidden in the homes. Relying on assumptions about the nature of building designs created increasingly unrealistic results.

Insurance carriers soon realized that home inspections were becoming less cost-effective as well as less reliable. Too often, the complex features of newer homes remained hidden from the inspection process if a square-foot cost was assigned and elements of remodeling were difficult to fit into the model; the limited amount of data used to create a square-foot estimate also precluded identification of salient features of more complex dwellings.

The character of the housing stock across the whole United States was changing, and, clearly, home valuation tools would become obsolete unless they changed as well. The industry defined the requirements: a new valuation methodology that could literally price building replacement cost from the ground up in a *simple to learn and use process*, one that would replace the legacy square foot approach, and one that would also take into account:

· The unique and evolving characteristics of individual buildings, inside and out

· Differences brought about by local economic or changing regulatory trends

· Mixed construction

· Dynamic cost data that fits multiple levels of more complexity

· Cost data that creates a building block approach to valuation so is able to address a wide range of home styles and features

· A variety of upgrades, enhancements, and features

· Localization beyond 3- or 5- digit ZIP or postal code segmentation

· Continuous change that was ongoing in the construction market

· The skill of end-users, most of whom would not be construction experts

· The core knowledge of the homeowners themselves, who could reveal the detailed characteristics of the property if questioned properly

The newly introduced computerized component-based systems met all these needs. They eliminated the implicit averaging and subjectivity associated with square-foot and unit-count estimating methods. One of the common complaints with legacy methods involved errors associated with totally subjective choices of class and quality. The new component approach virtually changed subjective input to observable and salient real home characteristics.

For instance, the majority of the square-foot methods made an overall assumption of the interior finishes in a house based on its perceived quality of construction. Therefore, all average 2,000-square-foot houses were implicitly assumed to have identical finishes (see Appendix 2 for a discussion of these assumptions), which by the 1990s was seldom the case. It may have been simpler to develop quality-based models, but the methodology became flawed given the reality of modern homes with their mixed construction variables. Clearly, because homeowners insurance is based on like-kind indemnification, it became important to be able to identify more of the internal and external features to properly value specific properties rather than fit them into hypothetical models.

The subjectivity of less-exacting valuation methodologies also caused value distortion. For example, construction class and quality were often confused with *condition* and *state of disrepair*. A property that had not been well maintained was often judged to be at a lower quality level. However, because the insurer could be required to replace the property with *new* materials of the same grade, condition and the state of disrepair became irrelevant considerations in the loss adjustment process.

Total component estimating systems overcame these inadequacies by focusing directly on the material and attendant labor used in the property, without regard to such subjective variables as class, quality, or opinion. The materials themselves dictated a property's cost. Additionally, total component estimating treated the interior of the property as equally important as the exterior. Therefore, wall material, as well as floor coverings and the like, became an important part of the estimate, with the result being a more complete and accurate valuation. That homeowners who live in these structures are able to identify the necessary ingredients for estimating added a degree of policyholder involvement anticipated when the first homeowner policies were born.

The Total Component Approach

The total component method was significantly different from square-foot and model-based methods because it priced a building in the way a professional estimator, quality surveyor, or contractor would. However, the complex formulas and extensive databases needed to perform the calculations were invisible to the user since adaptations in computer technology and database management overcame the user's lack of sophistication as well as the sheer size of the database. Using this method, insurance companies and their agents working with policyholders even on the phone could calculate a building's replacement cost within seconds, inclusive of all of the hard and soft costs of construction associated with properties in a single location.

To illustrate how the total component system works, consider one subassembly only—interior walls. The system first determines the makeup and size of the trade crews required to assemble and erect interior walls. The system then determines the number and type of components (e.g., studs, gypsum board, doors) needed to complete each subassembly (i.e., wall section), recognizing the *local* costs of each of the building components, based on all characters or digits in a postal code.

At the same time, it calculates the number of hours required by each labor trade to complete and erect each subassembly. Next, the program looks up the local hourly wage rate for each trade and multiplies the number of hours required by each trade by its hourly rate of pay, the result being the cost to rebuild that particular structure (interior walls, in this example) in its specific location. By performing similar calculations for every subassembly in the building, the total component system is able to quickly and accurately provide complete, detailed estimates of the entire structure.

Figure 3.1 and 3.2 illustrate the detailed nature of the total component approach.

Figure 3.1

Building Description: 1,350 Square Foot House in Augusta, Maine 04330

Total Component Method
Interior Walls, Doors, Studs, Gypsum Board, Doors

Labor

	Crew:	Hours Needed	X	Local Labor Rate	=	Labor Cost
	Carpenter:	(17.6 hours)	X	($14.39/hour)	=	$253.26
Studs	Laborer:	(17.6 hours)	X	($12.02/hour)	=	$211.55
Gyp. Board	Carpenter:	(55 hours)	X	($14.39/hour)	=	$791.45
Doors	Carpenter:	(20 hours)	X	($14.39/hour)	=	$287.80
						$1,544.06

Material

	Quantity Needed	X	Local Cost	=	Material Cost
Studs:	(1485 Sq. Ft.)	X	(.28/sq. ft.)		$415.80
Gyp. Board:	(4146 Sq. Ft.)	X	(.24/sq. ft.)		$995.04
Doors:	(7 doors)	X	(103.60)		$725.20
					$2,136.04

Total Labor and Materials for Interior Walls:	$3,680.10

A Case for Reconstruction Cost

Replacement cost estimating remained the centerpiece in the underwriting process, with increased emphasis in the 1990s. Fundamental to the new form of estimating that emerged however, was the inclusion of *reconstruction cost* data, which ultimately became the industry standard for improved risk assessment. At the time, Marshall & Swift and E.H. Boeckh each debated the merits of replacement cost, which had served the industry well, versus reconstruction cost.

Analyses of thousands of total loss claims paid by insurers, also known as Plateline studies, revealed a number of salient factors contributing to post-loss costs that were not addressed in a replacement cost valuation. These analyses clearly demonstrated the need to calculate insurable value inclusive of all expected post-loss costs. This insurable value would more appropriately represent what a carrier might be expected to pay following a loss and would also determine the proper premium for the actual risk insured. That insurable value was *reconstruction cost,* defined as the cost to construct, at current prices, an exact replica of the home, using like kind and quality materials, construction standards, design, layout, and quality of workmanship, and embodying all the home's deficiencies, super-adequacies (extra or excess quality) and obsolescence. Reconstruction cost also included site-specific and process-related costs, many of

Figure 3.2

Replacement Cost Analysis

J. Smith   Your Insurance Company
1 Main Street   99 Ninth Street
Augusta, Maine Anytown, U.S.A.

A-Z Agency
11 South Street
Hometown, U.S.A.

September 28, 2005   Policy No. AZ-12345

2-Story Residence
Anywhere, U.S.A.

Description	Total Amount
Foundation	$2,936
Slab on Grade	1,059
Framing	10,361
Roof Cover	1,762
Exterior Walls, Doors, Windows	15,798
Interior Walls, Doors	3,680
Wall Finishes	2,845
Flooring	5,058
Ceilings	2,824
Equipment	4,176
Heating/Air Conditioning	5,532
Plumbing	5,421
Electrical Systems	2,649
Total Replacement Cost	$64,101
Less Exclusions	
Excavations	324
Foundations Below Ground	2,612
	$2,936
100% Insurable Replacement Cost	$61,165

them *soft costs*, commonly experienced when rebuilding *after* a loss. Some examples include

- · Loss of economies of scale

- · Limited site mobility

- · Utilization of specialized repair and restoration contractors

- · Debris removal

- · Fees and permits

- · Building codes

- · Time urgency

It was also noted that the usual sequence of events in construction might often be altered when reconstructing after a loss. Generally, retrofitting repairs to existing building components was common, requiring greater skill to achieve and resulting in a loss of productivity associated with new construction.

As the industry moved closer to capped policy limits, making certain that the policy limits included all of the costs faced when losses occurred became even more relevant. Carriers that made the strategic decision to adopt *reconstruction cost valuation* data as the base Coverage A limit and used the formula

Replacement (Reconstruction) Cost x Rate = Premium

achieved greater capability to protect consumers, an offset to the loss of guaranteed coverage, plus the addition of premiums commensurate with the entire risk assumed.

Valuation methodologies that did not, and still do not, account for those additional yet very real costs leave the industry underserved and perpetuate a climate of underinsurance.

Soft Costs and Component-based Estimating

Historically, as today, whether for new construction or reconstruction, construction costs were typically characterized into two groupings—*hard costs*—largely direct labor, material, and equipment oriented, and *soft costs*—fees charged by a general contractor for construction services provided, such as supervision, overhead, and profit.

Hard costs are typically higher in a reconstruction environment than in new construction, due to such factors as economies of scale; tighter, less efficient scheduling (due to the carriers' desire to minimize temporary living expenses); higher trade skill requirements; higher workers compensation rates; access problems; and other factors.

Similarly, soft costs are also higher in a reconstruction environment. Contractors charged what current market conditions would allow, which is often the normal or equilibrium price, because across time supply generally adjusts to meet demand. But as the demand for contractor services escalated in a reconstruction environment, so did the fees that were charged; the magnitude of any increase was related to actual demand compared to relative supply.

The duration of soft cost increases could be short or long-term, depending on the circumstances behind the spike in demand. A local catastrophe such as a tornado generally had short-term effects on soft costs; they usually returned to normal or equilibrium once immediate rebuilding needs were addressed. In booming economies such as resort or other high-worth areas, market conditions allowed contractors to charge higher fees long term. These additional soft costs were not limited to the general contractor; a trickle-down effect also affected the fees charged by subcontractors, suppliers, and providers of ancillary services and were passed through to the building's owner.

Some of the less obvious soft costs included architects' fees, debris removal and disposal, the need for more sophisticated project managers, and the variances in general contractor and subcontractor profit and overhead percentages.

Because the insurance industry was and is in the business of replacing former existing structures, not building new ones in the more efficient environment of development construction, the component-based replacement cost estimating systems anticipated this situation and included the appropriate costs for it.

Risk-specific Construction Issues and

Component-based Estimating

Component-based estimation systems were very well-suited to enable the user to better determine costs in unique situations, such as homes built on hillsides. The problems associated with estimating costs for this type construction were highlighted after the Oakland Hills fires of October 1991. Many of the homes there were built on hillsides, and the severe underinsurance these policyholders experienced pointed to the inability of simple square-foot methods to address such site-specific situations.

While the homeowners insurance policy covered the cost of foundations below ground, policy language assumed that, even after a fire, the foundation would remain to be used in the reconstruction process and thus need not be included in the insurance-to-value determination. But this was not true in Oakland. Due to the intensity of the fires, many foundations were ruined, while others needed to be replaced because they no longer met current building codes. The average assumptions on which the valuations were calculated left homes undervalued, meaning homeowners were underinsured and carriers were not receiving premium commensurate with exposure.

Some of the more advanced square-foot methods attempted to use a single factor to calculate the impact of hillside construction on a home's replacement cost. Unfortunately, as is many times the case, using a simple solution for a complex problem too often led to unacceptable levels of inaccuracy.

To address this issue, the component-based estimating systems allowed the user to enter information about unique construction features, such as hillside construction. The replacement cost estimate was then built considering the labor and material costs necessary to replace such construction in each unique situation. The user input was simple; the computer handled the complex calculations, considering items such as the slope of the ground, site access, and ground type (rock versus sand, for example).

The component-based systems incorporated the intelligence of GIS (geographic information systems) technologies. By recognizing the location in which they are developing replacement cost estimates, GIS technologies propelled construction cost localization far beyond 3- or 5-digit ZIP code segmentation. The component systems could take into account appropriate building code information and consider relevant construction assemblies for dealing with heavy snow loads, heating and cooling requirements, frost depth, wind and fire conditions, and seismic zones (see Appendix 1 for a more thorough discussion of these factors).

This behind-the-scenes data assimilation made it possible for insurers to reflect dynamic, risk-specific cost information on individual dwellings, where previously they were hampered by the static nature of square-foot charts.

In the past, the insurance industry did not feel compelled to expand beyond the scope of square-foot and unit-cost methods for valuing homes because the many risk-specific requirements discussed in this chapter were not as significant as they are today, nor was the technology available to deliver fully integrated solutions. As computer technologies advanced, the insurance industry was able to take advantage of more risk-specific valuation methods. These actually paralleled the segregated approach with the advantage that the computer became a major part of the process, making new approaches easier to learn and use. In the current environment, the expert is now the component-based estimate system, not the inspector.

Experience has shown that by using these more sophisticated systems, replacement cost values varied from earlier methods, often increasing coverage limits. This was due to features of component-based systems that enabled collection of detailed interior and exterior features and finishes as well as the fact that these systems calculated the *reconstruction cost*, not new construction cost as in earlier estimating methods.

As carriers moved to component-based estimating in the early 1990s, Marshall & Swift's experience with numerous carriers, involving hundreds of thousands of policies, was that 73 percent of all main street American homes were undervalued relative to true replacement cost, and such undervaluation averaged 35 percent per home. Since that time, by adapting total component methodologies, insurance companies have been able to more accurately value new risks insured as well as update their books of business. Current research shows that the undervaluation problem has improved across the industry that has generally embraced the new methodology. In the United States we now recognize an estimated 58 percent of homes undervalued by an average of 21 percent. (Currently in Canada, which has not fully embraced component-based technologies, overall undervaluation statistics are estimated at 84 percent of residential properties undervalued 27 percent.)

Figure 3.3

Improvement in Residential Undervaluation* As of September, 2006		
Year	% U.S. Homes	% Undervaluation (average)
2002 and prior	73	35
2003	64	27
2004	61	25
2005	59	22
2006	58	21

* Source: Insurance to Value Quality Index™
© 2006 Marshall & Swift / Boeckh, LLC

Amelioration of the undervaluation problem has enabled the industry to realize significant benefits, including

· millions of dollars of previously unidentified premiums that have been recovered each year through adoption of total component estimating,

· added support provided to policyholders and the associated marketing value this brings,

· reduction in regulatory oversight,

- reduced Errors and Omissions exposure,

- lower operating ratios, and

- more leverage with reinsurance providers.

Ultimately, homeowners policy writers embraced total component property valuation methodologies because these methods overcame valuation challenges presented by more complex, less homogeneous housing stock. They also facilitated the ability to price on a risk-by-risk basis.

The fact that each insured risk was based on its unique characteristics gave policyholders a sense that the premiums they paid were based on *their own houses*, not on some abstract factors based on broad averages. Coverage limits and resulting premiums for these unique properties were also easy to explain and defend because the details upon which the value was calculated were typically archived in these systems. Because homeowners were most often the source of this information, they related to it well. This was not usually the case with the old square-foot brochure methods.

The addition of new approaches to replacement cost estimating became a catalyst for change in how books of property business would be managed. Since 1999 especially, the industry fully embraced the component approach, which required new focus on the overall underwriting process. The revolution did not stop there, as carriers took a fresh look at other business strategies:

- New restrictions on coverage, including the introduction of capped policy forms

- New higher deductible options

- Limited coverage for furs, fine arts, money, and jewelry under the homeowners forms, with additional coverage available via endorsements for additional premium

- Carrier-specific policies replacing ISO forms

- Replacement of third-party vendor rate plans in favor of company-specific plans

- Recalculation of coverage limits using valuation tools instead of less-sophisticated indexing programs

- Introduction of peril-based and risk-based rating

- Addition of credit as a measurement of risk desirability

End Notes

1.   Remodeling Activity Indicator for Fourth Quarter 2005; January 13, 2006; Joint Centers Housing Studies at Harvard

2   R05-1: The Changing Structure of the Home Remodeling Industry, Joint Centers Housing Studies at Harvard

Chapter 4

Building Cost Valuation
Guaranteed Replacement Cost Policies

The core elements of the homeowners policy have remained consistent since the introduction of the policy in the 1950s. Nevertheless, the definition of replacement cost has evolved. While insurers extended the basic homeowners policy to include many more perils in their policies, courts have interpreted various nuances of the definition of replacement cost. The courts typically expanded the policy's definition under the principle that one party—the carrier—controls the language, and the other party—the insured—must accept it.

The current standard policy language affecting coverage states that full replacement cost (up to the policy limit) will be paid at the time of loss if a policyholder maintains coverage limits of 80 percent or more of the dwelling's full replacement cost. In its earliest forms, replacement cost was the amount of insurance needed to restore the damaged structure to its state before the loss occurred. Technically this interpretation suggested a value equal to what was present before a loss—no more, no less. Therefore, if a roof was worn, a policyholder would not receive the full value for a new roof, but rather the amount that it would have cost to replicate the roof as it existed prior to a covered occurrence.

This interpretation of replacement cost often led to disputes between the parties, which in turn led to involvement by the courts. So, in an effort to minimize the legislative impact on the definition of coverage, and to assure that adequate coverage levels were maintained, insurers began to offer the "guaranteed replacement cost" endorsement.

A second catalyst for the development of the guaranteed replacement cost policy followed the mass merchandising practices of the past and was influenced by the financial circumstances affecting carriers throughout the country. In the late 1970s, interest rates were at double-digit levels. These high rates offered carriers the opportunity to earn substantial income by maximizing their premium levels, since premiums earned could be invested at very high interest rates. This cash-flow underwriting strategy continued to fuel market expansion, but often, as we would later learn, at the expense of sound underwriting.

Gaining greater market share, including a myriad of new marketing options like guaranteed replacement cost, was part of the strategy to build an increased capital base for investment. Because loss frequency was low, especially in comparison to recent times, interest in acquiring more market share by established firms was high. At the same time, nontraditional parties like Sears, ITT, Citibank, Xerox, and others eyed the property insurance arena with interest, opening an era of acquisitions and further fueling the mandate for penetrating new or existing property markets.

While guaranteed replacement cost has great merit when proper underwriting controls are practiced, without these controls it holds great risk. With guaranteed replacement, the carrier fulfills its obligation to the customer to insure a risk properly and indemnify the insured at time of loss. Moreover, since the endorsement requires that homeowners agree to insure their properties to their full proper value and pay premiums commensurate to the risk, everyone wins. Why, then, had it been such a disaster, ultimately to be replaced by an intermediate program—capped policies?

The immediate result for the property business when guaranteed replacement was introduced was a marketing and public relations bonanza and an actuarial time bomb. For only a few extra dollars per year, any policyholder willing to insure his or her home at the policy's inception for what was assumed to be 100 percent of its replacement cost, permit an annual adjustment in limits in accordance with construction inflation, and notify the insurance company of any new addition or alteration resulting in a percentage (usually 5 percent) increase in the dwelling's value would be guaranteed complete replacement in the event of a covered total loss, regardless of policy limits. This endorsement even had the additional impact of circumventing the 80 percent requirement of the policy's loss settlement provision. The carrier agreed to replace new for old, even if, following the loss, it was learned that the amount of insurance carried was not only less than the required 100 percent, but closer, say, to 50 percent or 60percent.

The implicit assumption by the carriers was that their agents would use the square-foot estimating tool to insure properties to their full replacement cost. Thereafter homeowners would be required to accept an annual increase in coverage to reflect the impact of construction inflation. This program was expected to keep coverage limits current and implicitly assumed the home itself never changed.

For consumers, the program was ideal, and for some elements of sales and marketing within the industry, it provided a new, though short-lived, competitive edge to close more business. However, as the industry came to learn, without controls in place, at least two fundamental pitfalls were inherent in the endorsement.

Policy Pitfalls

First, homes are long-term assets that experience a certain level of dynamics. They are systematically modified, remodeled, and upgraded by their owners. Over longer periods of time, the cumulative effect of this process is considerable. Most of these changes that affect the cost to replace a dwelling go unreported and are only realized when coverage is found to be inadequate at the time of loss.

In the 1990s, changes to properties made by homeowners increased overall replacement costs by as much as 3 percent per year. Today, the increase is closer to 7 percent. These increases occurred as a result of the dynamics in the North American housing market and the trend toward remodeling rather than buying new. The demographics in the United States support a continuation of this trend into the foreseeable future, a noted in Chapter 3. As a policyholder changes his property by adding a deck or remodeling her kitchen, he is adding insurable value and thus needs additional coverage. While a carrier is entitled to an additional premium for this exposure, it often goes unreported. Because neither the sales force nor the homeowner has a great incentive to report construction upgrades, the system of providing guaranteed replacement cost had a built-in bias against the insurance industry.

Second, the square-foot valuation tools in use could be manipulated very easily. These valuation tools relied heavily on the user's judgment of a structure's class and quality. Using these systems, one could easily modify one's judgment on the class of a structure and effect as much as a 30 percent swing in a property's replacement cost. This methodology itself could create a conflict in goals between the best interests of the carrier or underwriter insuring a property and those of an agent primarily charged with the generation of new business.

Sales and marketing channels within insurance organization would, with regular frequency, downplay the necessity of properly reflecting the replacement cost value needed to properly insure homes. The concept that the insured didn't really need to keep coverage limits current because "the carrier would pay full replacement cost anyway" was commonly discussed during the period.

As we later learned, a build-up of under-valued properties was occurring simultaneous to carriers expanding their homeowners coverage to include many more perils than the original homeowners form contemplated. These conditions led to an increase in loss frequency, which undermined premium adequacy and increased insurers' combined ratios.

Strategies to improve business ratios involving large rate adjustments emerged in the new millennium. However, with the high degree of regulatory oversight the industry faces, attempting to work with rate alone as a strategy was (and still is) difficult. Additionally, the science of ratemaking is predicated on the fact that measurements of exposure are indeed accurate. Therefore, even if an insurer were to successfully file a rate increase to cover an underwriting shortfall, if current exposures are not understood or are undervalued, there is no guarantee this change would, in the end, be sound, let alone saleable to customers. What is simpler to manage and explain is adequate *replacement cost*; and the key determinant of replacement cost, insurance to value, is an area that carriers *can* manage with customers, agents, and regulators.

Figure 4.1

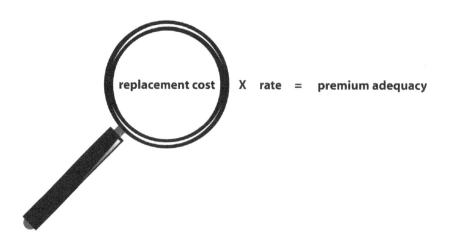

Of the two factors determining premium adequacy, replacement cost and its key determinant, insurance to value, is most easily managed by carriers.

Coverage Caps

After the catastrophes of the 1980s and 1990s, companies were asked to make good on their promise to replace homes under the terms of the guaranteed replacement cost endorsement. The catastrophes hurt homeowners insurance providers financially and, in many instances, led to failures. The era between 1988 and 1997 saw a large number of insurance companies fail, property insurance being the culprit, and owners like Sears, Xerox, and ITT that had purchased insurance entities for cash-flow advantages vacated their holdings.

As a result, there was a flurry of activity by homeowners policy writers. They looked to find new ways to *cap* replacement cost options in order to reduce the overall risk they insured. At the same time, carriers struggled to find cost-effective means to revalue their business and adjust pricing to reflect the overall risk they insured. An increasing number of carriers went full circle, back to limited coverage to find ways to once again cap their exposure. However, their efforts met with resistance.

For instance, after the Oakland Hills fire losses, the California Department of Insurance reviewed guaranteed replacement cost coverage terms and addressed caps on overall coverage amounts. This review indicated that while the insured clearly has an interest in the property (and, therefore, an interest in developing the coverage amount), if agents and companies choose to cap the amount of coverage, they also must help the insured establish an adequate replacement cost at the time the policy is issued.

Over time, many legal decisions have addressed who should be the party responsible for gathering the information necessary to establish replacement cost or actual cash values on insured buildings. The reality is that an insurance company must know the replacement cost value they may pay out at the time of loss, or their ability to calculate and generate adequate premiums is limited.

Pricing Issues

At the time that the concept of insuring to value appeared in the 1960s, the primary concern centered around the issue of valuing homes insured in the policy under Coverage A, then pricing (rating) the homeowners policy based on the assumption that Coverage A was correct. Although the onus had once been on the homeowner to provide valuation information to her insurance carrier, it was believed by many in the industry that consumers had no real understanding of the value of their structures or the pricing variables that determined their rates. Given the choice, consumers uneducated to the implications of underinsurance would tend to understate values to achieve a lower premium and save money. It was also easy to lower the rate structure and thus the premium paid. The insurance-to-value process, therefore, needed new technologies that could access alternative databases to verify rating variables as well as building replacement costs. The concept of insurance to value ultimately requires an accurate assessment of a home's replacement cost. To that valuation, a rate can be applied that reflects the carrier's risk based on the home's location, likelihood of burning (i.e., wood frame vs. masonry construction), proximity to a water supply, geographic claims history and numerous other variables.

Indexing

While insurance carriers were using simple replacement cost tools as part of the mass merchandising process, the renewal structure for policy issuance required some means of establishing an up-to-date value on buildings when policies were renewed. Therefore, carriers needed to have some method for bringing policies up to date on a year-to-year basis. It was essential that this methodology work within the companies' existing technology and the constraints of their business management capabilities. To this end, publishers of replacement cost data developed ZIP- and postal-code-specific *index* factors that could be applied to current coverage on the insurance companies' entire books of policies in force.

An index works by representing an average change in residential construction, weighted for an area of the country (typically at the three-digit ZIP- or postal-code level). This variable would be multiplied by coverage limits to come up with new coverage amounts. Because this is a simple calculation, insurers were able to renew policies by multiplying the factor against the then-current coverage amount. The resulting value was then used to issue a new premium amount and to use the new Coverage A amount for the coming year. Regrettably, no consideration for the added value of remodeling construction was made unless the insured or agent notified the carrier.

The catastrophes of the 1990s led to a realization that a number of insured properties with customized or intricate features were neither accurately represented in the original valuations nor accurately updated over time. After all, a building with elements such as hillside construction, major glass exterior walls, or older home construction requires a higher degree of expertise to reconstruct than a simple home with limited features. Naturally, if the structure were inaccurately valued to begin with, indexing the value over time will not solve the problem.

Advantages of Consumer Participation in the Valuation Process

In the beginning, the onus of establishing insurable value was placed on the insured— both when policy was first written and at the time of loss. With mass merchandising and the advent of guaranteed replacement cost coverage, carriers essentially assumed the role of determining coverage limits at the point of sale, then with each renewal. Companies equipped staff and agents with cost-estimating tools from third-party publishers. These publishers also provided carriers with construction inflation increase factors known as *indexes*. Over time, legislators and the judiciary continually pressured carriers to accept the burdens of responsibility in the event coverage limits were inadequate. Numerous court cases placed the burden of coverage clearly on the carrier as they ruled that a carrier must understand what it insures. In some cases, the insurance companies were held culpable for not establishing or maintaining adequate value and then refusing to indemnify the insured completely, and they were ordered to pay full replacement cost of the properties and, further, to pay punitive damages.

Insurance carriers, feeling vulnerable after the major catastrophic losses of the late 1980s and early 1990s, therefore began to consider new ways to update coverage limits for the properties they insured. The question for carriers became: ***"Who can best provide home characteristic information?"*** The answer was *the homeowner*. After all, homeowners live there and can best answer questions about home characteristics that affect valuation. Most homeowners are more than willing to participate in the valuation process when properly approached, especially after witnessing the destructive and economic impact the many hurricanes, fires, earthquakes, and terrorist acts unleashed on the United States after 1989.

As might be expected, field inspections were also found to be less accurate than homeowner-provided information in the measurement of a home. Consumers, rather than inspectors, are often better able to identify the style of their homes and provide more accurate information regarding the details of the property. Furthermore, it was found that inspectors were seldom able to get inside the properties they were hired to inspect and, when they were able to get inside, they used the square-foot tables the carriers provided rather than producing a component-by-component estimate. Although carriers had been putting a downward pressure on the price they were willing to pay for inspections in an effort to contain costs, the inspection process continued to be viewed as uneconomical for the industry. As a result, it made sense to use homeowners as a primary source when gathering this kind of information.

One advantage carriers have found in involving homeowners in the process is their active buy-in to the result. By providing the details on their own property, they are able to see direct correlations among the information they provide, the valuation of their property, and the premium that they are asked to pay.

MSB has completed a number of studies involving many thousands of homeowners. These results have shown that, when queried in a carefully scripted manner, homeowners can describe the important characteristics of their homes, including size, to reliably capture the necessary input to determine proper coverage. Simultaneously, as homeowners provide input into the process of determining adequate coverage, they arguably assume some responsibility for the replacement cost. This, however, has not been adequately tested in the judiciary system.

Both the insured and the insurance company benefit from an accurate replacement cost valuation that involves policyholder input. The acceptance of the valuation by the insured improves since the insured is directly involved in the process. The insured is fully covered at the time of a loss, and the insurance company earns premium commensurate with the risk.

Once homeowners realize that carrying adequate insurance is based on the accurate valuation of their property and involves their direct interest in protecting their property assets, most are willing to aid in the valuation process. However, this still leaves the carrier with the problem of individually valuing large numbers of homes by correlating vast amounts of owner-supplied data.

That problem can be addressed by pairing homeowner-provided information and a computerized total component-estimating system to create an advanced integrated system capable of providing the most accurate valuation of residential properties. This total component process is, in fact, an electronic return to detailed estimating. The difference is that today the computer, not the user, does the bulk of the work.

The results, when transmitted electronically to the insurance client or agent, allow for automatic policy updating. Because all interior and exterior building characteristics are archived, a home's replacement cost is easily reprocessed each year to increase coverage as needed. With the risk-specific data, changes in material and labor costs specific to each property are used to calculate a revised replacement cost for each renewal. This is a major improvement over indexing methods.

Outsourcing the Valuation Process

Like many other industries today, the insurance industry has sought outside help for recommendations to help improve profitability. The nation's premier consultants have often recommended that carriers reengineer, downsize, regroup, and restructure their business. They have also recommended outsourcing, or reliance on external resources to provide work originally performed in-house, to enhance the overall profitability of any business. Outsourcing benefits those carriers that cannot fully focus on developing unique applications themselves or that find the costs of accessing state-of-the-art technologies they need prohibitive. Outsourcing to experts enables the carrier to be continuously up to date, because it becomes the mandate of the provider, not the carrier, to stay current.

Outsourcing also allows a company to focus on its core competency and turn its non-core requirements over to other firms that specialize in these areas. For example, carriers regularly use third parties to have their phone systems installed and maintained, because telecommunications is not the focus of insurance companies; they may also use an outside payroll specialist, which is cheaper and more reliable than processing payroll internally.

Outsourcing reduces the need for internal overhead such as skilled personnel and automated systems that have continuing needs for maintenance and development. Vendors of outsourced functions have to maintain and enhance these same types of resources and need skilled personnel to maintain their competitive edge against the customers' alternatives. Additionally, specialty businesses often have technology solutions their customers can never hope to learn or maintain economically.

Thus, outsourcing to experts can accomplish the needed business function and help improve the carrier's profitability. As we have seen, carriers have struggled with the problem of valuing and pricing homeowners business for over forty years but have found the problem overwhelming and, too often, they have failed. Insurance companies are simply not construction experts.

Now, with the new technology and added investment made by cost estimation providers, valuation companies like can assume all or part of the insurance-to-value process for carriers. Studies have shown that by using outsourcing to better manage this process carriers can reduce combined ratios for homeowners business by 10 points or more, as shown in figure 4.2.

By involving policyholders in the development of risk-specific, component based valuations, carriers will be able to regain profitability sufficient to provide, on a long-term basis, the financial stability and security their customers need and desire. New technology and outsourcing options provide solutions to financial and organization problems that have plagued the industry for decades. Solutions that include both an accurate replacement cost and a proper rate structure appear to be the needed combination for those carriers that will prosper in the 21st century.

Illustration of the results carriers have realized through outsourcing insurance-to-value processes to experienced third party vendors with proven home valuation and direct customer contact techniques.

The column on the left displays a typical company's results as reported by A.M. Best. In this example, the column on the right is based on these assumptions:

· Average policy premium of $400

· Minimal contact of an average of 70 percent of policyholders

· 73 percent of homes undervalued by approximately 35 percent

· Underwriting expenses estimated to increase at 50percent of previous rate

· Investment income assumed to remain at the same percentage of Premiums Earned after the increase

It should be noted that the primary expense associated with improving a book of business is largely a one-year cost. Thereafter, a modest fee is needed to keep information current (see Chapter 8) so that profitability will continue to increase in following years.

Figure 4.2

How Strategic ITV Programs Focusing on Policyholder Contact Helps Improve Carrier Profitability

	Carrier's Existing Pro Forma	Pro Forma AFTER Implementing Book of Business Initiative	
	A Typical Company's Actual Performance:	ITV Program's Impact On Performance:	Improvement:
Homeowners Business			
Net Premiums Earned	$117,978,000	**$135,287,732**	More that $17,309,732 in additional premiums (14.6% increase)
Losses/Adjust. Expense	$101,697,036	$101,697,036	Losses are unaffected, but decrease as a percentage of premiums by 11.0 points.
ITV Program Expense		$3,539,340	Only 2.2% of premiums earned, and only a one-year expense.
Underwriting Expense	$35,983,290	$38,623,024	Increase is a result of increased premiums earned.
TOTAL UNDERWRITING EXPENSE	$35,983,290	$42,162,364	
Combined Ratio	116.7	106.3	A reduction of over 10 points in this critical ratio.
Investment Income	$2,949,450	$3,382,193	Investment income rises as premiums earned rise.
OVERALL OPERATING RATIO	114.2	103.8	
Income/(Loss)	($16,752,876)	($5,189,475)	HOMEOWNERS BUSINESS IS NOW ON THE WAY TO PROFITABILITY.
Total First Year Gain to Bottom Line:		$11,563,401	
FIRST YEAR PROFIT AND LOSS PAYBACK		4:1	
LIFETIME PROFIT AND LOSS PAYBACK		22:1	

Chapter 5

The Effects of Catastrophes on Replacement Costs

Catastrophes, from an insurance point of view, are occurrences that affect significant numbers of insured risks in concentrated areas wherein coverage is broadly provided for a single peril. In the homeowners market, a significant population of insured dwellings is ripe for adverse events, since in the last 20 years a large proportion of the U.S. population has migrated to coastal areas. Risk of loss in these areas from earthquakes, hurricanes, severe storms, or, sometimes all three, is high. These events affect housing stock more so than any other insured risk because of the ability of a single peril to give rise to a large number of claims.

Because catastrophes have had such a dramatic impact on the homeowners insurance market, they further reinforce the immediate need for carriers to adequately insure dwellings at the point of sale and thus obtain an amount of premium commensurate with the risk to be insured against. As discussed earlier, this need had been subordinated to mass merchandising of homeowners policies in a competitive market that accepted less-than-adequate limits in order to gain market share and revenue. The pattern of major catastrophes in the 1990s (see Appendix 3) strained reserves and threatened the viability of some carriers. Today, this pattern is being repeated in the wake of unprecedented property losses arising out of the 2004 and 2005 hurricane seasons, which, according to the Insurance Information Institute, have reached nearly $23 billion and $58 billion, respectively, as of this writing.

Delays and Cost Escalation

Catastrophes present unique major problems for both homeowners and insurance carriers. The costs to have adjusting and repair work done increase greatly in the aftermath of a catastrophe, and this is certainly not the only problem.

For insureds, getting contractors to do repair work promptly is very difficult. In catastrophe situations, local contractors often sign up enough work in two to three weeks to keep them busy for a year. Unless an insured is a friend of a contractor, a wait of three or four months or longer before repair work begins is not unusual. The use of out-of-town or out-of-state contractors can expedite work, but many insureds are reluctant to use such contractors for a very good reason: If an out-of-town contractor does not repair the home properly, the insured is likely to have a problem getting the contractor to return to correct faulty repairs. This concern further intensifies the supply/demand shortage of local contractors available to perform such work.

A second factor affecting repair following catastrophes is the escalation of repair prices to an unreasonable degree, known as "price surge". An increase in the delta variable of up to 40 percent from normal levels of building costs is common in such occurrences. When there is a great demand for work and very few contactors to do it, however, the economic theory of supply and demand comes into play, so prices too often increase, especially in the short term. Although this happens far too frequently, it is not considered to be a reasonable or fair reaction to the circumstances. Those contractors or suppliers that abnormally increase their prices should be asked to explain the reasons for the unusual increases.

Repair work prices can always be analyzed. An installed price is a composite of labor cost, material cost, and the subcontractor's and general contractor's mark-up for overhead and profit. Occasionally, a heavy equipment cost is involved, but this is unusual, since most reconstruction work is done with small tools and equipment. The need for heavy equipment is normally only encountered on very large losses or total losses.

For example, in September 1992, Hurricane Iniki severely damaged dwellings and commercial buildings on the Island of Kauai, Hawaii. Immediately prior to the storm, a subcontractor's price to install ½-inch standard drywall was $0.85 per square foot. With the general contractor's mark-up, the price quoted by general contractors was $1.00 per square foot. Within thirty days after the storm, many general contractors had increased the drywall price to $2.25 per square foot and more. The drywall contractors, in the interim, had increased their price to $1.00 per square foot. Had the general contractors marked up the post-storm drywall contractors' price by the same percentage that they marked up the pre-storm price, the general contractors' post-storm price would have been $1.18 per square foot, not $2.25 per square foot. With the $2.25 per square foot figure, the general contractors' post-storm mark-up for overhead and profit was 125 percent, a rate completely out of line. This was a classic example of contractors taking advantage of both the public and the insurer in a very bad situation. Figure 5.1 outlines the makeup of these changes.

Figure 5.1

Subcontractors' and General Contractors' Prices Following Hurricane Iniki
(per square foot)

	Before the Storm	After the Storm
Drywall, 1/2" Standard (Material)	$0.24	$0.24
Drywall Workers ($20.00 per hour)	0.40	0.50
Drywall Contractors' Markup (33%)	0.21	0.26
Total Drywall Contractors' Price	0.85	1.00
General Contractors' Markup	0.15 (18%)	1.25 (125%)
	$1.00	$2.25

In order to analyze prices, the adjusters responsible for equitably handling claims must know material prices, labor rates, and rates of production. Fortunately, for those handling claims, computerized estimating programs provide that information. In the case of a catastrophe, it would be wise for users to ask those who furnish these estimating programs to provide before-and-after catastrophe prices. This historical information gives users the opportunity to compare before and after prices and question any unusual price increases. During the six months subsequent to the storm on Kauai, one vendor had to make six revisions to his program to keep up with continual price increases by contractors.

Similarly, in 2005, shortages of qualified contractors following Hurricanes Katrina, Rita and Wilma increased labor costs. For example, shortages of labor in concentrated storm zones meant that contractors had to pay wages at time-and-a-half or double-time. Because contractors and trades people were working six to seven days a week for ten to twelve hours per day, productivity declined. In addition, general contractors ended up paying room and board for out-of-state labor, which in the case of roofing alone, raised costs by $28 to $35 per square.

In 2006, MSB began tracking price surge in the United States at the 5-digit ZIP code level to actually report the delta caused by post-catastrophe demand (See Appendix 3). Because demand varies based on proximity to the most serious damage, localizing the price surge for affected labor and materials is clearly necessary. While this kind of data is new, it supports insurance companies and public entities with information they need to better understand cost and to control unnecessary severity, if not fraud.

Additional Claims Expense

Insurance companies incur a major expense from the reopening of claims files. It is one thing to reopen a file because covered damage was missed, additional damage occurred, or one or more of the contemplated methods of repair was inadequate. It is quite a different situation to reopen a file because prices increased between the time an agreement was reached with the insured and the insured's contractor and the time the work was actually started. Insurers have no realistic control over this. Lengthy delays may occur because the contractor was unable to start work promptly or because the insured elected to make changes in what was to be done. The cost of reopening a file is not just the added cost of the loss, but it also is added to the time required to revisit the loss site, write a supplement to the estimate, and renegotiate the settlement. Time is money, and far too much time has historically been spent during catastrophes reopening files for the wrong reasons.

Underwriters should know which types of dwellings are subject to heavy damage from catastrophic perils. In areas where most hurricanes occur, dwellings, in particular, are not as well constructed as they are in moderate and cold climates. On Kauai, most dwellings were wood frame with corrugated galvanized roofing. This type of dwelling is at great risk of heavy damage when the wind reaches 100 miles per hour.

The Northridge, California, earthquake of January 1994 presented different problems. Dwellings and buildings were for the most part not totally destroyed, but there was considerable foundation damage. In some cases, houses had to be lifted off their foundations so that the foundations could be repaired. The greatest difficulty was determining the extent of damage and what needed to be done to repair or replace damaged buildings. Actual price increases were not as great as those experienced in Kauai. Fortunately, there were a great many contractors in the Los Angeles area who were helpful to both the insureds and insures from both competitive and reconstruction standpoints. Work could be started as soon as an agreement was reached on the scope of damage and the price to do the work. Structural engineers and consultants (most of whom were contractors or former contractors), working in concert with claims representatives, were able to resolve questions regarding structural damage and the cost of making needed repairs. Here again, computerized estimating programs were very helpful to those involved in determining the amount of damage to dwellings.

Preparing for More Profitable Results

An analysis of the property industry following the catastrophes of the 1990s estimated that catastrophes contributed as many as 10 to 15 points to the 125 average combined ratio experience in those years. Underinsurance problems resulted in the industry losing 10 to 15 percent of its premium income on its normalized business. Absent some benign and forgiving turnaround of events, this means, at a minimum, even without catastrophes, that if carriers are unable or unwilling to properly reflect the appropriate replacement values on their books of business, they can fail.

A similar financial impact occurred again following the 2004-2005 hurricanes and the wildfires and tornadoes of those years, with some major property writers vacating territories or setting up subsidiary plans. Even with the major rate increases of the early 2000s, the problem of underinsurance soaked up underwriting profits, because, as we have learned, rate-only strategies do not cure underlying problems which are too often revealed when it is too late to change them.

However, the industry should avoid the temptation to focus on catastrophes as the root of the insurance industry's financial difficulties. The catastrophes of the past few years served to highlight problems in homeowners insurance that have been on-going. With increasing regulation in those states where a catastrophe either has occurred, or is more likely to occur, adapting data to conditions *following a loss* becomes a continuous game of catch-up.

Over a decade ago, as a February 1995 article in *Claims* magazine reported, reliance on older technologies to value buildings and establish coverage limits at the point-of-sale had been significantly discredited. Today, this message is seconded by the NAIC and individual state departments of insurance, as discussed in Chapter 9. An approach that links coverage determination more closely to the construction activity that will be performed is now receiving the highest visibility. It is also coming center stage when rating bureaus establish the rate score for property writers. At this time, total component valuation systems are the only methodologies that satisfy the regulatory mandates for both point-of-sale property valuation and loss-adjustment techniques.

It is difficult for insurers to keep abreast of technological upgrades needed to adjust to the changing dynamics in the home construction market. Each catastrophe presents its own set of problems for the claims adjuster. Outsourcing the estimation and construction portion to experts who continuously enhance the systems needed is an option that frees adjusters to handle more claims.

The industry must reach a conclusion as to what can be done from an insurance-to-value viewpoint to offset the increase in catastrophe-related rebuilding costs. For example, even though it is untenable to incorporate these relatively infrequent occurrences into standard property valuations, it is appropriate to build these factors into the potential endorsements or new policy pricing models for catastrophe-prone areas, as well as into reinsurance. If the pundits are right about increasing hurricane activity and severity or the next California earthquake being "the big one," the insurance industry can no longer afford the luxury of a delay.

Chapter 6

Special Conditions—Emerging Markets and High Worth Homes

Over time, evolving economic and construction trends underscored inadequacies found in legacy valuation systems, while positioning the benefits of component-based approaches that helped users mix and match components to fit each new situation. As new layers of complexity were introduced in home construction the number of lower end housing units dropped while the number of what would formerly have been unique, top-layer homes grew. The strong growth in remodeling also added to this shift as homeowners essentially turned low-end homes into more upscale properties. Furthermore, builders of new developments were less likely to provide basic home packages when more lucrative upgrades could be sold.

As a generality, residential replacement costs that averaged lower than $100 per square foot prior to 2000 would be in the minority thereafter. Naturally, replacement costs of homes increased as fixtures and appointments were becoming increasingly more diverse. Attempting to fit modern homes into estimating models that assumed homes were homogeneous became obsolete.

Insurance professionals began to adopt what eventually became a proliferation of modern estimating techniques. But in selecting among these modern techniques, two critical criteria needed to be addressed. Since legacy valuation methods were not only inherently inaccurate but also could not adapt to market changes, whatever technique was chosen needed to be flexible enough to accommodate future changes in the residential construction market. Second, because legacy valuation methods were often inadequate to meet the demands of a growing insurance business, being constrained by both manually intensive calculation processes and limited paper-based formats, any system needed to be robust enough to meet the volume demands.

Insurers therefore were justified in evaluating whether component based methods could evolve, where legacy valuation systems could not. They found that, unlike the model-based programs of the past, modern component-based systems were and are truly flexible and, when coupled with today's advanced automation technology, provide both the efficiency and scalability to address business demands.

Gauging the Impact

The rapid change to the construction landscape that began in the 1980s that we have described has not abated. Builders and consumers are not retreating towards basic homes; instead, they are exploring alternatives in existing markets and making entrepreneurial advances in non-traditional spaces, such as the development of coastal, hillside, and mountain resort homes.

There are now millions of these nontraditional properties in books of property business written in the era when homes were homogeneous in design within their economic cells. Therefore, at the same time that the changing construction and homeowners marketplaces necessitated the use of modern estimating tools, they caused insurers to examine more closely their books of business to determine if their understanding of these books was indeed accurate. Since their understanding was often a product of the use of legacy valuation systems, it became important to review their books in order to understand what risks may be hidden and where geographic changes affecting the book had occurred.

As a result, from 1999 to 2005, many insurance companies, understanding the value of modern estimating technologies, actively pursued the question of the makeup of their homeowners' business, undertaking updating projects in part or in whole intended to address:

- hidden details in the files,

- coverage or premium adequacy, and

- conversion from legacy approaches to modern component solutions.

In particular, MSB participated in book of business revaluation projects for nearly fifty property writers in order to help facilitate conversion from legacy square-foot methods and to improve operating ratios, rating models, and consumer protection. As described in later chapters, this revaluation process, as much as the invention of total-component estimating, helped insurers improve the percentage of undervalued homes from 73 percent of homes undervalued by 35 percent in 1999 to 58 percent of homes are undervalued by 21 percent today, a dramatic and important improvement.

Changing Economic Cells

Prior to their revaluation projects, the majority of property writers believed their books of business constituted a broad mix of residential housing types of average construction. However, as insurance companies looked deeper into the business they some discovered that books of business were often organized, intentionally or unintentionally, by niche markets (old homes, high-worth properties, or substandard housing). Others, however, were surprised to find that what they thought was a broad mix no longer fit the assumed residential profile that they had made part of the original marketing campaign. Instead, their property book was comprised of a diverse mixture of housing types and values.

This diverse mixture occurred not only from the changes to the construction and remodeling trends previously cited, but also as a result of a new phenomenon: the fact that economic cells where homes were being written had changed. What insurers discovered, based on their own internal analysis and by MSB working on books of property business with them, was the fact that new cost concerns affecting the overall ITV process were emerging, with distinct and often sophisticated variations in local economies.

New Economic Cells

Since 1996, the economy blossomed and consumers relocated, impacting replacement costs in ways that might not be obvious. The economic cells where homes were situated impacted the claim costs insurers would pay and, therefore, the sufficiency of premiums collected, independent of raw costs of construction. The industry discovered that ITV became area-dependent, and carriers needed to include in the ITV calculation such considerations as:

- large concentrations of very upscale dwellings within larger communities, with concentration of high worth housing having a direct effect on contractor mark-ups;

- new, tightly aligned markets that were often missed in existing rating territory tables;

- soft costs that were being charged due to complex site access, building on hillsides (not just in California), and demands for stringent code compliance;

- layers of added contractor overhead;

- subtle modifications to home construction resulting from code changes following natural disasters in selected communities;

- costs of transporting supplies to less accessible but also populated areas;

- refinancing initiatives by lenders in select communities with associated increases in home remodeling;

- regional laws concerning debris removal and associated expenses for rebuilding on damaged sites;

- proximity to hazards at the site; and

- large numbers of affluent buyers in concentrated areas affecting buying power and contractor rates.

ZIP and Postal Code Alignments

In 1998, Farmers Insurance Group called attention to the fact that geographic segments connected at the three-digit ZIP code level actually contained many sub-communities that were affected by one or more of the above considerations and that should therefore be regarded as distinct for construction and valuation purposes. The 2000 United States Census underscored this change. The census identified and research by MSB verified a significant number of distinct construction pockets within three-digit ZIP code segments, counties, or even cities. This further confirmed that differentiation of markets at the traditional three-digit ZIP code level does not reveal the true picture of home construction around the United States. This observation also holds true in Canada.

For example, part of Maricopa County, Arizona, (the county that includes Phoenix) segment is identified by ZIP codes beginning with the three digits "853." However, as seen in figures 6.1, 6.2, and 6.3, these same three digits also begin the ZIP codes that encompass Yuma, a more rural community over 200 miles southwest of Phoenix, the desert areas surrounding the northern Phoenix community, and pocket communities of upscale areas like Glendale. These communities should be considered differently than Phoenix for valuation purposes because of the substantial and significant variances in construction characteristics and costs within them.

Figure 6.1

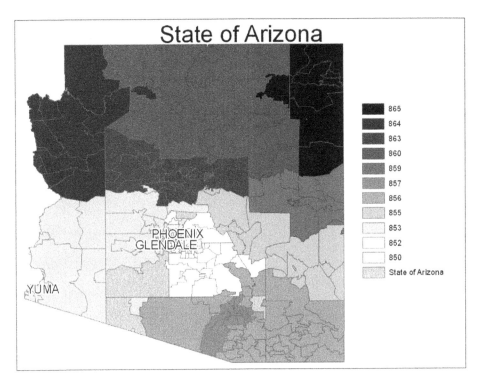

Figure 6.2

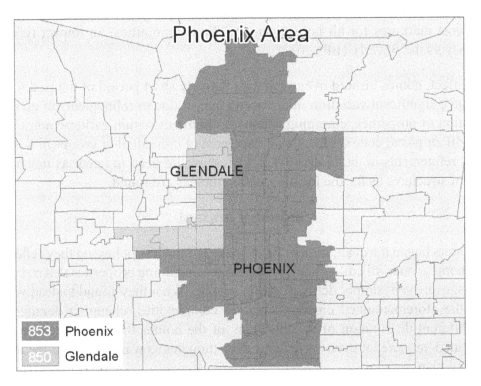

Figure 6.3

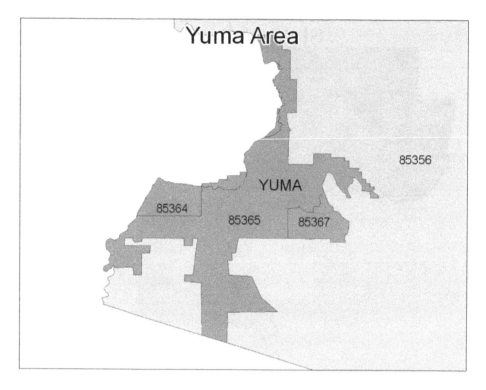

Pocket communities that are dominated by high income housing have grown exponentially since 1996. The economic impact has been to push up hidden costs, such as soft cost mark-ups for all housing in specific communities, an impact referred to previously as the Beverly Hills effect.

In effect, homes insured over even the relatively short period of the past ten years might have significant variation in replacement cost due to refinements in geographic distribution of properties, emerging economic segments within earlier county level or 3-digit ZIP or postal code segments, or placement of individual or groups of homes. As a result, refinements in the modern ITV process would need to occur as much for the variety of structures as for the locations where homes are found.

Industry Impact

Insurers began the evaluation of their books of business believing they reflected an earlier, homogenous mix of ordinary construction containing properties that represented on average an even, simply defined market profile. What they found instead was that, due to the aforementioned emerging market complexities, changing demographics, and a different distribution of wealth, many of the homes they insured were instead complicated, *upscale*, or even *high value*, even though this was not part of the intended marketing plan.

In fact, MSB's Analytics Research Department performed a study in 2005 that revealed that of the ninety insured books of homeowners business reviewed, a majority was not as normative as company executives assumed, having metamorphosed into a combination of home types, value ranges, and conditions. (See Figure 6.4.). For carriers, the immediate impact of this was felt on the renewal process. As discussed previously, simply updating coverage limits by applying index factors universally to all risks in a large geographic segment, without periodic review or revaluation of the existing book, in too many instances had the effect of missing essentials of the home and its associated market. Instead, insurers needed to adopt more active book of business management programs to uncover true book composition and address market changes, as is detailed in Chapter 8.

Currently, as explained in Chapter 7, with millions of policy records passing through modern component methodologies whereby properties are now able to be archived in accessible formats unheard of before 2000, analytic review of books of homeowners business have allowed insurers to uncover unique book-of-business profiles. They have begun to identify homes whose replacement costs are influenced by more factors than previously considered throughout their geographic distribution, inclusive of changing home characteristics profiles, concentration by age of construction, size, code variation, mark-ups, and other elements that were not present when the first version of *Insuring to Value* was conceived. What was thought to be a book of so-called main street dwellings in a certain market segment might actually have large concentrations of nonhomogenous properties and hidden cost considerations such as those mentioned earlier in the chapter.

The ultimate result has been the need for increased vigilance on the valuation front, a continued need to monitor and include other components in the replacement cost calculation, and the need to provide valuation tools that address variation and further support the work performed by each end-user. The valuation systems insurers choose today should incorporate the flexibility that legacy systems did not, permitting the addition of new cost variables at the component level as needed and as market conditions further change. This flexibility must be an integral consideration in the estimating software used by insurers and their clients who might not be construction experts.

Figure 6.4

Distibution of Properties in a Book of Business

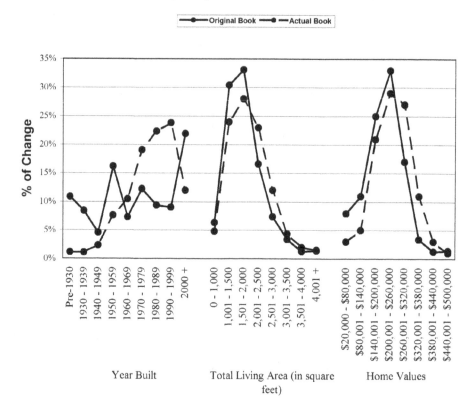

| Year Built | Total Living Area (in square feet) | Home Values |

Effect of Emerging Markets on Book of Business Profiles

The profile of a carrier's book of business will change over time. The line graph on the left represents change in construction age, the line graph in the center represents change in Total Living Area, and the line graph on the right represents the change in replacement values. Sophisticated valuation tools enable carriers to track these changes so book profiles can be strategically realigned to meet company goals and objectives.

High-Worth Dwellings

Standard designs inclusive of the expected main street home styles, mobile-manufactured housing, condominiums, townhouses, and other similar styles are still relevant structural types today.

However, the growing numbers of truly upscale and/or high-worth properties emerging in clustered subsections of larger communities or as stand-alone dwellings bear new scrutiny.

As the 1990s changed to the new millennium, categories of homes referred to as custom built would take on new meaning to contractors and consumers alike, with units of the new housing stock looking more like mansion-grade structures than like tract developments (See Appendix 5). Homes became larger and contained many specialty features and upgrades, were irregular in shape, and made use of modern appliances, protective systems, and fixed covering fixtures unheard of in earlier periods. It was also not uncommon for these homes to be built in excess of 4,000 square feet of Total Living Area, with large spans of open space and associated roof lines that needed additional support or superstructure. As buildings became larger and carried the weight of more finishes, seemingly revisiting the ornate workmanship of the pre-1930s era (but with modern materials), the framing, foundations, and other supporting construction variables needed for these properties were required to scale accordingly.

Because these structures have a wide variety of components that all too often make them one of a kind dwellings, it is less likely that they can be valued through use of generalities or standard cost methods. When using the total-component approach, databases to enhance the valuation program's ability to import appropriate cost values for these unique structures, especially when located in specific high-worth sectors, would be required. Since users of estimating systems would find it increasingly difficult to identify the needed component parts of these buildings, as well as deal with the other code and soft-cost variables pertinent to communities where they tended to cluster, the effort associated with valuing these properties would begin to shift to estimating systems using advanced database management techniques and automation supporting modern insurance-to-value initiatives. The component approach needed to become more sophisticated, actually learning through use of artificial intelligence architecture, so that it could adapt to this dynamic environment, taking into account that approaches used to value main street type structures lacked the sophistication, engineering, and cost variables necessary to properly value upscale or mansion-grade homes.

That modern estimating systems were already component-based by design was an advantage. They already contained the application systems necessary to select and include cost components needed to value alternative kinds of buildings. Nevertheless, it was now necessary to introduce second-tier calculation engines to take into account and value new building complexities.

Equally important, these additional systems needed to be able to be deployed and used in a way that presented an efficient workflow to the end-user. Therefore, these second-tier calculation engines would run seamlessly underneath simple to learn-and-use input screens, enabling the software to support end-users more effectively by automatically including the widest range of home styles, interior and exterior feature and finish options, mark-ups, localization factors, code impacts, architectural variables, and engineering requirements for users. Further, it would be inadequate to simply add greater numbers of input items to a main street home calculation engine to attempt to calculate high-worth dwelling estimates. The engineering for 7,000 square foot homes with similar features and finishes used in 1,800 square foot homes would not support this simplistic logic, which is in fact reminiscent of the by-gone era of the square foot brochure that assumed a straight-line correlation between increased size and increased value.

Rather, as we have shown, the cost of truly high-value homes increases in a manner not exclusively correlated to size but, instead, to the actual quantity and quality of features, fixtures, and construction methods. Therefore, comprehensive use of architecturally sound formulas and associated pricing was needed, inclusive of unique construction features as outlined in the discussion of high-value homes in Appendix 5.

As valuation systems evolved, particularly from 2003 to the present, MSB used modern automation techniques to introduce multistructural estimating engines that value, in a seamless input process, both main street and upscale homes, mansion grade homes of any size or value, mobile manufactured housing, condominiums and townhouses, island and mountain resort construction, brownstones, and other structures. These technologies use interchanging calculators that users never see but that work for them automatically based on input supplied. These engines, all "total component" by design, actually shift estimates to the right calculation routine automatically, freeing end-users to focus on collecting basic input generally known and understood about homes. At the same time, by using modern database management techniques that have evolved since 1999, the system applies the proper overhead and profit, code-compliant items and regulated features of debris removal, and architects' costs and substructures associated with the layer and type of construction involved. These engines apply construction line items and costs at the closest local level, because of the large numbers of new and emerging markets that are today subsets of what were originally 3-digit and 5-digit ZIP code segments.

MSB has also undertaken extensive research on the U.S. and Canadian home construction markets, highlighting more than 3,000 specific ZIP code segments out of the 43,000 that exist in the United States alone, where economic profile and/or construction requirements (especially addressing upscale housing) have the effect of driving replacement cost values in unique ways not earlier understood. By isolating these market segments, insurers not only obtain better insurable values but also learn more about specialty and niche markets on which they may want to focus their marketing efforts.

Emergence of Distinct Economic Zones across North America

Figure 6.5

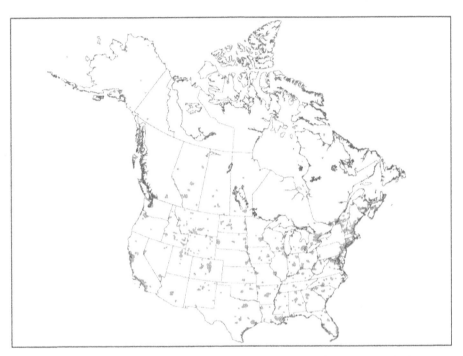

Because of thousands of new and emerging markets that are today subsets of what were originally three-digit and five-digit ZIP or postal code segments, modern valuation tools must be capable of providing construction line items and costs at the closest local level.

Chapter 7

Data Archiving

Concurrent Evolutions

When the first edition of Insuring to Value was published in 1996, it was the starting point of understanding the needs of insurance companies, their agents, and policyholders (and all others with a financial interest in real property) to become involved in property estimating. Just as important, the book addressed the very positive impact derived from not only integrating building cost estimating within the insuring process, but also from the estimating technologies that had evolved over time as the housing market changed.

That first edition dealt with the construction era following World War II and divided the timeline of home construction and insurance estimating methods into two essential categories: the era of similar construction (or a time when common tract housing emerged) and the era of mixed construction (or the era following the boom years of the Reagan presidency when residential construction once again became unique and varied). This latter period had the good fortune to occur along with advances in computer automation, which seemingly arrived when most needed. Advances in computerization techniques through the invention of such items as powerful personal or laptop computers, large-scale user networks, and, ultimately, the Internet made it possible to update insurance estimating protocols in a manner that would keep pace with the complexities in the home construction industry that evolved. Modern automation, with total component estimating, also made it possible to automate vast databases of building-block-level cost data as well as knowledge-based insights that enabled modern estimating systems to organize and reorganize cost data to fit (at local levels) multiple combinations of home types at the characteristics level for virtually every property risk.

The ten years since the first edition have proven the merits of a total component approach. However, we are again at a point where further complexities have entered the picture, necessitating that the industry build on the foundation that was established. These complexities involve a host of new, peripheral issues surrounding local building requirements (such as code refinements, unique mark-ups, and soft cost variables in localized market segments) that impact both new construction and reconstruction as well as the challenges of keeping up with changes in housing stock already on insurers' books.

Today, it is increasingly critical that insurers value their legacy business, or existing books of property business, with the same degree of certainty that they do new business. They should review, update, and revalue it through a total component approach. Addressing legacy business is a matter being driven not only by business necessity, but also increasingly by regulatory decree. Recent consent orders introduced in 2006 by the National Association of Insurance Commissioner (NAIC) members in several states, including Arizona, highlight the value and importance of attending to a *continuous review of existing business* in order to avoid misalignment between what is thought to be insured and what is found when claims occur. As described previously, the industry has updated coverage limits over time by applying indexing factors globally to legacy books when homeowners' policies renew. Nevertheless, as we discuss later, indexing alone does not uncover the unreported changes people make to their homes. The concern is that, although much has been done to improve the valuation process for new business, the preponderance of renewal business on carriers' books means that nearly 60 percent of residences in the economy are undervalued when property claims occur.

Fortunately, technology has once again evolved to the right place at the right time. The opportunity for automating the valuation process for both new and renewal business exists by combining the capabilities of component-based approaches to insurance to value with technologies like Web-hosting to add an important enhancement to book of business management—*archiving*. As we discuss later, this capability has even more far-reaching implications beyond the subject of replacement cost valuation and book-of-business updating. It enhances each carrier's competitive advantage in markets served by aggregating vast amounts of detailed home characteristics and other data in formats that lead to analysis of how each company looks and performs against the competition in similar markets.

Analytic Foundation

Not only did component-based estimating become the industry standard, but it also led to the collection of granular, easily verifiable interior and exterior home characteristics data about each risk insured that would ultimately be archived, or preserved electronically, when home replacement cost estimates were calculated. It also solved the problem of paper-based input that was too often lost or incomplete, as it was systematically replaced over time with modern, authoritative descriptions of properties organized on a risk-by-risk or *risk-specific* basis. Today's Web-hosted systems, used to estimate the majority of new business risks, also add vast data storage capacity at minimal cost. It permits simplicity in the process of collecting and saving for perpetual review all known data elements about homes in formats that can be easily accessed, retrieved, and changed.

This was not possible with the square-foot approach because that methodology did not address component parts of homes. Nor was it possible to change or archive characteristics in automated systems that relied on quality-based models because of the static nature of the models and the assumptions and calculations underlying their design. Even when new modeling programs are introduced that attempt to accommodate specified component items by adjustments to base models, the limitations of the methodology too often result in over or understating the adjustment impact, as MSB learned through experience with the now-retired Advantek™ valuation program. Perhaps because of lack of knowledge, simplicity of design, or lack of development resources, some new valuation tools entering the property estimating environment that emulate the approach used in Advantek develop cost estimates that jump radically when entering something as common as a new room or structural component. In contrast, adding or subtracting component selections to component-based valuation systems does not drive building costs to irregular levels either up or down.

Ten-Year Impact: Realizing Profitability and Policyholder Protection

Now that the total component method has been widely accepted, we have the added benefit of hindsight and the ability to examine historical results from industry and vendor entities that adopted the component plan set forth a decade ago. In fact, sustained use of the total component approach, especially where insurance providers worked to convert entire books of property business to the component methodology, including archiving of building characteristics profile data at the policy level, has actually surpassed estimates of financial and competitive benefits for insurers and their customers. Indeed, as depicted in Figure 7.1, the era from 2001 through the present was characterized by significant improvements in combined ratios in the homeowners' insurance arena. Although it can be argued that there were substantial price increases during that time which, of course, support financial improvements, there were clearly movements by large numbers of property writers to adopt the component approach for writing better new business applications. At the same time large numbers of property writers worked to convert their existing business to the component approach.

With ten years of actual experience behind us, the original argument posed in 1996 that stressed the value of implementing total component methods has not only been effectively proven, but also has led to a dramatic and measurable improvement in the undervaluation problem discovered in earlier decades. As mentioned earlier, as we close 2006, the number of single family homes in the U.S. economy that are estimated to be undervalued has dropped from 73 percent undervalued by 35 percent to 58 percent undervalued by 21 percent.

Figure 7.1

Change in Combined Ratio for Homeowners Insurers 2001-2004	
Year	Combined Ratio (excluding dividends)
2001	121.24%
2002	108.70%
2003	97.50%
2004	93.96%

Source: Highline Insurance Data

Component-based valuation impacted property insurers' bottom lines. The combined ratio for homeowners insurers improved more than 27 percentage points in the four years 2001 through 2004.

In addition to observing the overall improvement in industry operating results, MSB researched and analyzed more than four million partial loss claim files from 1996 to the present; performed *analytics,* or sophisticated data analysis, on nearly 10,000 total loss claim files referred to as *Platelines;* and analyzed the records resulting from updating nearly seven million legacy homeowners records in nearly forty books of property business. The analysis was heavily weighted towards day-to-day business, but it also included storm, fire, and other catastrophic events. The intent was to understand how component technology and data affected ordinary property business with normative construction trends versus trends found in stressed environments impacted by concentrations of loss with the potential for demand or price surge.

The research revealed to carriers, reinsurers, and rating agencies that the degree of severity in the combined ratio in books of homeowners' insurance business, especially as the percentage increased to triple digits, became a predictable measuring tool for the degree of undervaluation in a book of business. Therefore, the need to correct the problem became more urgent. The combined ratio was found to be directly related to the amount of underinsurance as well, and, at various break points, severity increased. Insurance carriers really needed to have combined ratios in the low 90s to be truly profitable, since even numbers lower than 100 percent could mean the insurer might not have adequate operating capital to reinvest in their business. As time went on, having underwriting expense higher than 32 percent of net written premiums and/or Loss & Loss Adjustment Expenses higher than 65 percent also suggested the need for remedial action in the business.

Insurers could use this type of research to gain insights into how their business was performing, as well as using it to trigger corrective action on a number of fronts—especially coverage adequacy. When coverage was inadequate, premiums charged might be inflated to cover losses incurred, thereby making insurers less competitive within the markets they served. At the same time, properly valued and maintained books of property business would have large premium pools so carriers could afford to offer the most competitive solutions and prices. As will be shown subsequently, the success of archiving property characteristic data across the industry also provided high-level trend information as a reference from which insurers could actually learn how they stacked up to the competition in local markets.

Specifically by adopting a modern approach to property estimating, the industry began to collect and archive data about the risks they insured. The immediate and long-term implications on the operation of the business as well as bottom line results included:

- improving overall operating ratios by at least 9 percent,

- gaining millions of dollars in new premium revenue every day, with the residual effect of establishing the new base of premium dollars for the business for the duration policies are maintained (average eight years),

- making insurance to value and ultimately performance in the book of property business more predictable,

- understanding risks insured at the component level long before losses occur,

- establishing an internal index for understanding the current state of insurance to value in each book of property business,

- collecting and maintaining details on every home insured in a permanent and readily retrievable archive, and

- strengthening market position, competitive advantage, and pricing adequacy in every market served.

Considering the value of total component estimating, insurers archiving data in modern databases address the changing housing stock they insure, reduce errors and omissions, and ultimately have the mechanism to stay closer to policyholders over time. As stated previously, with archived data collected about homes in the component estimating process, the objective nature of this data can be verified continuously with policyholders since it is information they understand about the place where they live. In fact, the discernable nature of the data collection process has proven ideal for updating books of property business directly with policyholders via the telephone, eliminating the need for expensive and time consuming field inspections that typically don't examine the interior of the house.

Furthermore, because underwriting must also manage the renewal book, the ability to collect information in detail on homes insured and then to archive the data for ongoing reference makes loss potential more predictable, uncovers those risks that contribute the highest combined ratios, and satisfies growing regulatory demands.

Focus on the Competitive Advantage

Insurance companies adopting total component methodologies and archiving have found that they increase their competitive advantage. Component methods enabled property writers to mix and match building blocks of construction in a manner unique to each local environment, thereby creating nearly infinite numbers of cost factors, rating tiers, and other variables that would enable them to uniquely underwrite virtually any risk insured from a single database. Rather than trying to fit homes of varying complexity into generic models and factors, insurance companies were now able to:

- remain in markets they might otherwise vacate,

- develop products and associated pricing for niche market opportunities others might avoid (i.e. coastal exposures, vintage home markets, high-value homes, mobile-manufactured housing, and so on),

- build marketing profiles for optimal niche markets based on book of business profiles and performance, and then find more in local economies,

- underwrite individual risks by applying regionally required discounts for such items as code compliance based on proven characteristics information collected, and

- recommend coverage limits based on readily understood and demonstrable building characteristics for particular homes, rather than average base costs inferred everywhere.

Today, an estimated 90 percent of U.S. property writers have adopted component-based systems for valuing the new property business they insure. Additionally, nearly seventy of the top 350 property writers have, since 1999, also made a concerted effort to convert their book of legacy records from older square-foot data to the component approach through book of business revaluation and/or other conversion programs. The advantages they received from modern component-based technology were due in part to the fact that these systems were designed to collect and *archive* data in ways earlier models that were essentially paper-based when first designed could not do. Revaluation and/or conversion overcame the previously discussed limitations that compounded problems in valuation over the life of an insurance policy. Capturing and ultimately saving, or archiving, essential home characteristics that drove replacement cost value was the breakthrough that was needed.

Evolution of Archiving

When component-based systems were first presented to the industry, they carried with them the essential technological advance of being able to finally capture and, equally important, archive salient information about homes. That the risk-specific data was easily accessible merely hinted at the great potential for building estimating systems to become even more valuable as underwriting tools.

Archiving data was an essential part of the earliest designs of component-based estimating. However, existing technology infrastructure did not as a rule accommodate efficient archiving. Legacy, mainframe, and disparate siloed systems limited the ability to compile the data collected in a central repository for general use by carriers and their agents. While component systems saved data, the data might be in the agent's computer, or on a company network server in a regional office. Additionally, the computing industry had only begun developing Windows™ applications, geocoding, and mapping systems, and the Internet was still in its infancy and not of practical use for everyday business. Therefore, while the first edition of this book provided the industry a first look at total component estimating, it would take a few years for the technology needed to most effectively use these estimating systems to become ubiquitous within the industry.

In addition to evolutions in the general technology marketplace, changes occurred in the cost-estimation vendor marketplace that made both component estimating and archiving a reality. In 2001, the leading building cost estimating suppliers Marshall & Swift and E.H. Boeckh merged, becoming Marshall & Swift / Boeckh, or MSB. Both companies had been working earlier from different points of view towards the introduction of total component estimating in reaction to market events discussed in previous chapters, but had actually come to similar conclusions regarding the efficacy of component-based methodologies.

While there have been many technology advances made since the first edition of this book, it was the development of the Internet and widespread adoption of Web-based applications that finally made data accessible to all interested parties, giving 24/7 access to mission-critical information for writing insurance policies and understanding risks after claims occurred. The evolution of the Web as a part of modern insurance-to-value programs also made it possible to better manage book-of-business updating through revaluation projects, as well as to keep coverage current each year as buildings changed. The Web also provided expanded platform capabilities for insurance companies to archive data in ways that carriers' legacy hardware could not. Through archiving and resulting analysis, carriers gleaned insights on how residential construction was proliferating around the nation due to economic growth during the late 1990s.

The ultimate result was technology that today gives carriers the ability to:

- manage books of property business profitably over time through Web services initiatives,

- perform important analytics functions on the book of business to gain deep insight regarding how the business actually functions and how it can be made more profitable and competitive, and

- marry claims experience with underwriting data to explore whole new frontiers of risk-based modeling and improved business development.

Growth of Web-hosting

As mentioned previously, carriers implementing component-based methods and seeing the benefits of insurance to value on new business soon realized the benefit of converting legacy information about homes insured to the component approach. As a rule, however, those carriers saw no easy or efficient way to do so because of the inaccessibility of legacy data. Even today, for instance, MSB estimates that detailed characteristics of nearly forty million homes are actually archived; however, the majority of this data is not accessible to carriers' policy management systems for various reasons, not the least of which is that many of the policy management technologies in place today are essentially the same core systems employed in the early 1990s. Those carriers' component estimating therefore is done through auxiliary systems that are the repository of archived information.

One solution to this problem is Web-hosting of archived data. Early experience showed that component-level data being managed for various insurers via an application service provider (ASP) site could in fact be retrieved, reviewed, and reprocessed as part of an active book of business updating project. This ultimately led to MSB's deployment of Web platforms on which valuation data could be archived.

Insurance companies, realizing that the data collected for homes they insured could be safely stored on Web sites with encrypted security and hierarchical access controls, asked for the ability to change and otherwise work with the data collected. Those carriers began using Web-hosted valuation and archiving technologies to manage books of property business from inception to renewal, ultimately creating a new evolution in the insurance-to-value process that proliferates today.

Currently, more than 230 property insurance companies are accomplishing some element of their insurance to value process on Web sites hosted by third parties, breaking the logjam for data access, management, and storage caused by legacy systems. That these same Web-based solutions are able to interface now with carriers' policy management systems via Web services and other electronic data interchange methods is a decided advantage and also shares resources where core competencies exist. The explosion in Web hosting also makes it possible to hold data for book of business review and updating, as well as more easily share data collected and maintained with the people who know the most about homes—*the owners.*

Other Advantages of Web-based Solutions

Today, carriers can have access to vast amounts of risk-specific information, including new replacement cost values and more, placed on secure, encrypted Web-hosted sites where each company underwriter, claims adjuster, or agent with authority can call up and download 24/7. The events and details of each building valuation can also be shared easily with insurance consumers whose property was reviewed. This is critical, because in the past when questions or debates arose about the nature or extent of detail surrounding each calculation, agents and company personnel would defer to a paper record that might have been kept in a remote location, if at all. With Web-hosting of detailed, component-level property data, the record and all manner of calculation and detail is available whenever and wherever the insurance professional needs to present it. Because storage is also relatively inexpensive, building large data files has been simplified. And, because Web-hosted applications require little or no internal information technology (IT) support from insurers, as well as limited or no interface with carriers' legacy systems, proliferation of these new data management processes could occur.

That insurance companies continue to request additional services on these sites is a further testimony to their willingness to outsource major portions of insurance to value initiatives. Functions that in the past required IT or other internal support are now outsourced, including home replacement cost calculations for new and renewal policies, field survey work, policyholder communications via a variety of media including mail, email, or telephone, and other book of business management tactics. The net result is that carriers can remain focused on their core competencies of managing insurance transactions, writing policies, and overall policy management, rather than dedicating valuable resources to these support services.

The Web provides still another advantage that is even more far reaching. Companies like MSB are capturing, storing, and providing not only data used in the valuation process, but also vast amounts of claims and other home-site-specific data. As we will show, this type of data has enabled carriers to accomplish several strategic objectives outside the traditional insurance-to-value process, including streamlining their claims adjusting procedures. Additional objectives include demonstrating to actuaries and underwriters new levels of risk-specific information that can be modeled for such tasks as risk-based or peril-based pricing, increasing accuracy in the risk selection process, creating alternative property scores that are alternatives to credit-only models, and designing policies tailored to their customer base.

Archiving and Analytics

The reality that insurance analysts, relying on the newly archived data for managing strategic initiatives and competitive pricing models, could now understand risk concentration by home type at the characteristic level to better understand risk concentration for reinsurance or catastrophe modeling ultimately set the stage for comprehensive analytics on books of property business.

Considering that modern component-based insurance to value technologies made dramatic improvements in the valuation landscape from inception, the by-product of these programs is now being realized. Today more than 50 percent of homeowners' risks have received a component valuation and nearly 70 percent of these have actually been archived. MSB, for example, has more than twenty-one million homeowners records archived in a total component format through its Web-hosting solutions provided to property writers in the United States, with the remaining homeowners risks hosted on carrier-based systems.

As part of the ultimate data collection process, extensive validation procedures evolved resulting in best practices guidelines all could adopt and defend. In the case of MSB, leading members of the U.S. insurance industry participated in the development of several data validation programs to derive an analytics-based best practices initiative that gave birth to standards already codified by state insurance departments, as discussed in Chapter 8. The validation program included the collection of nearly 20,000 actual total loss files to bench-line ITV systems requirements and verification, the continuous review of home survey information to model the current market profile in five-digit ZIP code segments (and beyond), and the ability to overlay claims experience with the stored characteristics of homes underwritten . This validation project not only proved systems and data viability for the estimating process but also paved the way for the development of underwriting analytics, which further laid the foundation for better alternatives to indexing and book of business management, benchmarking of individual carrier's books of business versus consolidated industry data and, ultimately, for specialized risk-based modeling.

Archiving is also the basis for other strategic activities insurers undertake. By creating an archive of components that can be mined as well as analyzed against other data sources, an archive allows companies to develop actionable business intelligence on which they can base both strategic and tactical decisions.

For example, MSB studied 100,000 properties that had been valued using a component-based approach and for which both values and component information had been archived. Data on those properties was combined with data on the types of perils that had produced the greatest claim frequency over four years. The resulting analysis led to some definitive, and unexpected, findings.

One of the surprising findings of this analysis related to hail losses in a sector of homes built in the 1980s. Homes of that era built with vinyl siding had a significantly higher frequency of hail losses than vinyl-sided homes built in other decades, approximately 46 percent versus only 19 percent. In effect, owners of vinyl-sided homes built in the 1980s were and still could be having their hail premium subsidized by other policyholders.

Figure 7.2

Indexing Impact			
Example:			
Current Coverage Amount:	$100,000		$100,000
Adjustment Factor Index	x 1.03	Avg. Adjustment from Remodeling	+ $10,000
Updated Coverage Limit	$103,000	True Replacement Cost Before Trending	$110,000
		Trending Update	x1.03
		Minimum Required R.C. Limit	$113,000

From this perspective, we see the following impact occur if insurance companies simply index the book year after year using the prevailing methodology.

Companies can use this type of business intelligence and translate it into actions for establishing underwriting criteria, setting rates, making product changes, or developing new marketing strategies. Over time and with better data that allows more insight, they can reduce subsidization and create a narrow band around the true rate for individual risks. This not only allows companies to target more profitable accounts but also allows them to charge more accurate premiums, which is more equitable for individual policyholders.

Underwriting opportunities afforded by capturing, archiving, and analyzing component-level property detail include:

·   uncovering common traits within individual or groups of policies that are underinsured,

·   identifying policies or groups of policies that have a high hazard exposure that the carrier's regular, individual-account underwriting process did not reveal,

·   identifying policies that have incorrect or missing information, such as being placed in the wrong rating territories, and which can be targeted for corrective underwriting action,

·   performing market segmentation analysis based on property size, style, age, location, or other characteristics to uncover strengths, weaknesses, and other trends by segment, and

·   comparing books or segments of books of business against industry benchmarks.

Additionally, technologies such as standards-based data interchange that enable integration of data from third-party providers have made deeper analysis easier for carriers. Examples of site-specific data that carriers now have at their disposal include:

·   materials, components, and labor for all postal codes up to the present time,

·   historical loss data on individual properties and surrounding properties,

·   postal addresses geocoded into latitude and longitude coordinates,

·   hazard data such as brush fire zones and distance to the coast geo-coded to individual properties, and

·   industry-wide property econometrics and demographic information.

This information can be combined with data from a carrier's own property book to provide underwriting insights, such as unacceptably high value concentrations in certain areas or other segment- or book-level problems.

In addition to providing the basis for data mining and supporting decisions at the book-of-business level, archiving also has value at the individual policy level. Creating and maintaining an archive of interior and exterior features for every property insured and then regularly sharing this information with policyholders meets several important business objectives, including:

- discovering where changes in home construction have occurred before losses occur,

- giving insurance consumers more involvement in the insuring process for their specific properties,

- identifying the true base line for coverage on an annual basis, and

- eliminating the need for reunderwriting or revaluation projects that can damage company-agent-customer relationships.

Archiving: The Bridge between Underwriting and Claims

Capture and archiving of data can pay dividends beyond underwriting. In particular, if carriers can merge granular-level property data from the underwriting process with claim data, they can use this consolidated information to make better decisions in both underwriting and claims.

There are many different methods by which carriers tackle the issue of consolidating data. They may build a data warehouse devoted solely to analytics and into which data from underwriting and claims systems is loaded; they may create a master data source that serves as the single source of customer data for both operational and analytical data; or they may take other approaches.

Which approach a carrier chooses is dependent upon many underlying technological issues, including the number of siloed systems and data sources, data format issues, the cleanliness (accuracy and completeness) of existing data, and other considerations. More important than the method, however, is the fact that today's data transformation and integration technologies provide insurers with tools to solve the problems that often made such integration previously difficult or impractical at best, and often cost-prohibitive or unworkable at worst.

Specific analytical opportunities within the claims area that are supported by archiving valuation and home characteristic data include:

- identifying individual claim cost items that deviate from industry norms,

- comparing individual claims adjusters and offices,

- identifying claim severity (total cost) drivers that consistently escalate the cost of claims,

- summarizing losses by market segment and feeding this information back to underwriting so that pricing, products, and marketing can be adjusted, or

- identifying best practices improvements to ensure claims are settled accurately and quickly.

Finally, archiving can be important not just for claims analytics but for handling open claims as well. For instance, an underwriting archive of property characteristics made accessible to claims adjusters can assist in valuing damaged property as well as when comparing assertions made by claimants with information provided at the time of initial application.

However, none of these activities, or those discussed in the next chapter, is possible unless a foundation for analysis is laid by archiving property component and valuation data at a granular level of detail.

Chapter 8

Managing the Ongoing Book of Business

Just as we saw following the fires and storms of the late 1980s and early 1990s, events like the California and Kelowna, Canada, wildfires (2003) and Hurricane Katrina (2005) brought attention once again to the question of coverage adequacy in the homeowners insurance market. This time around, two new themes that were missed in the 1990s emerged that were not only widely discussed, but also led to a series of strongly recommended action steps referred to in wildfire hearings held by the California Department of Insurance as *ITV Best Practices.*

What U.S. insurance regulators in particular identified as important considerations in the aftermath of recent catastrophic events included the following considerations:

- The viability of closer interaction among insurance providers, agents, and policyholders to manage sustainable coverage limits for every property risk insured. Because it was clear that modern insurance to value programs are now designed to accept relevant property characteristics input from a variety of sources, the question of proactively involving homeowners in the valuation process was defined.

- Increasing focus on maintaining coverage adequacy long-term in books of property business by institutionalizing procedures for continuous recalculation of replacement cost values for policies on the books, effectively developing a book of business management process for sustaining coverage and premium adequacy in a way that is measurable.

The outcome of meetings held by the National Association of Insurance Commissioner (NAIC) since the 2003 wildfires, as well as messaging from public hearings in states including California, Arizona, New Mexico, Louisiana, Mississippi, and Florida, underscored the importance of determining proper insurance to value when policies are first written. As important, the meetings set a new standard of concern regarding what should be done to better maintain coverage adequacy as policies mature on the books.

Following the era of Hurricane Andrew, the California earthquakes, and the Oakland Hills fires, focus revolved around development of better valuation systems and data for use in the sales process to get coverage right when polices are underwritten. However, in the aftermath of more recent catastrophic events, and in consideration of the fact that most companies are now equipped with the necessary valuation systems and data, it has become clear that what was needed was a modern approach to address *legacy* business that may never have been reviewed since policies were written. This suggests that moving to a more precise, component-based approach to valuing existing homeowners' business should be a major consideration, if not a required undertaking, by homeowners carriers.

The fact that undervaluation still occurs as often as 58 percent of the time and by an average of 21 percent, suggests the need for additional analysis and action to find and correct outstanding business issues affecting property business. As is discussed in this chapter, attending to updating coverage limits within the existing book of property business with the same degree of intensity applied to review each new insurance policy is now a practical concern and one that, when handled effectively, yields increased policyholder protection, higher retention and customer satisfaction, and obvious financial rewards. In addition, by helping protect consumer assets more effectively over the term that insurers maintain homeowners policies, regulation is less likely to occur and the remaining barriers to sustained profitability, coverage, and premium adequacy is expected to be realized.

Introducing Best Practices Strategies

As discussed previously, construction costs change, consumers remodel their homes, and market segments evolve, all of which put pressure on insurers to consider the long term impact these and other factors have on insured housing stock. During the 2005 San Diego Fire hearings hosted by then California Insurance Commissioner John Garamendi, the California Department of Insurance worked with carriers and data providers to better understand what the industry faces over the lifetime that policies are maintained. Their goal was to develop realizable solutions that would be implemented in order to avoid undervaluation when total losses occurred. The result of this investigation had profound implications because it led to a strong, sometimes regulated requirement that a new model for maintaining coverage adequacy over time (referred to in California as *best practices*) be implemented within the insurance industry. The intent was establishing and maintaining proper insurable values for the lifetime of a book of property business, inclusive of the participation by everyone involved in the insurance to value equation—including agents, carriers, and the homeowners themselves.

Through the medium of the hearings, Commissioner Garamendi outlined a process for eliminating undervaluation and associated consumer complaints through adoption of a continuous effort to update and recalculate coverage limits, beginning when policies come onto the books and continuing at the time policies renew. Important to the process, which was also adopted by other NAIC members, has been a scripted and regular dialogue with homeowners about the current characteristics profile for each property insured. The most critical of these recommendations state that carriers should:

- Obtain a reliable, component-based estimate for each property insured,

- Perform risk-specific valuations that do not incorporate short-cut methods or quality judgments,

- Archive information gathered for continuous reference over time,

- Confirm the information gathered about properties with homeowners when policies are first written and continue to reaffirm the information on a regular basis with the consumer,

- Ensure that the valuation program utilized is founded on actual claims experience, and

- Recalculate values annually rather than applying inflation indexes to policy limits.

California State Senator Jackie Speier also held hearings in 2005 devoted to the issue of underinsurance in homeowners business. Following up on consumer complaints after the Cedar and Paradise wildfires of 2003, these hearings again confirmed the need for a consistent, longer term view of insurance to value and also looked into the proper use of replacement cost tools when agents and consumers meet to conclude a property insurance transaction. Of interest was the fact that industry critics suggested insurance agents could be using software that simply applied a few pieces of home characteristic data to develop insurable values when policies are first written. Such data is sometimes collected from outdated or incomplete tax record sources or prior policy review, from limited review of actual home characteristics profiles, or assumed in other ways, leading to potential underinsurance problems that would carry through the life of policies maintained on a carrier's books. The question of establishing insurable values through use of so-called *quick-quote* methods of estimating was dismissed as inappropriate since a minimum number of input items are essential to adequately describe a property in terms that would be defendable in the valuation process. (Refer to Appendix 2.)

Overall, three important points evolved from the California hearings that ultimately impacted the way other states and the NAIC itself looked at insurance to value:

- Component-based estimating software works when properly used.

- "The detailed (ITV) questionnaire leads to valuations within spitting distance of actual loss." (George Kehrer, Consumer Activist).

- Component-based estimating systems "appear to be extremely useful and extremely accurate." (Commissioner John Garamendi).

Best Practices Advocate Cited by Insurance Regulators

The recommendation by independent sources of the modern *best practices* model that incorporates component-based estimating highlights the practices and disciplines necessary for proper insurance to value. These best practices complement the proposal submitted to the industry in 1996, that which was outlined in the first edition of *Insuring to Value*. MSB concurs with the tenets of best practices and has demonstrated through statistics amassed over the past ten years that they are valid and achievable. Not only the letter, but the spirit of the best practices model should be practiced in the way business is done, with the overall mission of establishing and maintaining the most protected and profitable property business for all involved. Also, validation of any estimating process used must be based on total-loss claim experience, which is, ultimately, the only demonstrable verification process.

In addition, MSB further advocates collection of more data elements than were the norm when the square-foot models were popular, especially when these items are easily observable and understandable and can be obtained in most instances from homeowners themselves. For instance, as detailed in Appendix 2, MSB recommends that thirteen salient characteristics be obtained for each property insured when a component-based valuation method is used. These characteristics include not only expected information regarding location, age, and size details, but also details on types and extent of finishes, fixtures, and any additional items that make homes unique, such as fireplaces, hillside construction, professional kitchen upgrades, and other details that can be obtained through the use of open-ended questioning.

As an example of a successful insurance provider that has already adopted this model, California Insurance Commissioner John Garamendi praised the Interinsurance Exchange of the Automobile Club of Southern California during the state's mandatory hearings following the 2003 wildfires. In the San Diego hearings, Mr. Garamendi reviewed the practice of collecting component-level information as part of the carrier's insurance-to-value program for new and renewal business. Equally important, the insurer was recognized for reviewing the information for clarification with policyholders, not only when risks are first written but *also at renewal*. Inconsistencies were identified and corrected collaboratively, resulting in policyholders being better prepared for loss events and the carrier's better able to maintain premium adequacy.

Although the Interinsurance Exchange of the Automobile Club of Southern California was specifically cited, the best practices identified by NAIC leaders had, in fact, already been delivering advantages for insurance carriers that had adopted these concepts independently over the preceding two decades. On the east coast, one insurer that adopted the concepts much earlier was able to provide double-digit dividends for homeowners business in a coastal state many property writers regarded as challenging at best. These two successes stand in direct contrast to the results experienced in a line of business that, for many insurers at the same time period, produced unprofitable results, triple digit operating ratios, and some business failures. Incorporating a *best practices* model like the one described herein and as these carriers did offers immediate, demonstrable benefits as part of modern insurance-to-value process. By so doing, carriers gain the advantage of:

- Increasing homeowner participation in the insurance-to-value process, which not only benefits all parties involved, but enforces an original mandate of the property insurance form,

- Finding and correcting errors in coverage throughout the lifetime policies are maintained,

- Providing a continuous review or audit check on coverage amounts,

- Remaining current with remodeling and upgrades policyholders make to their homes,

- Measuring premium adequacy risk-by-risk or across whole market segments,

- Achieving vast amounts of very valuable information confirmed between the carrier and policyholder, and

- Eliminating consumer complaints, thus reducing the need for governmental oversight by providing greater transparency into the insuring to value process.

In addition to reaping the positive financial rewards already discussed, carriers adopting the best practices model can also reduce governmental involvement. While it is certain that policyholders are better able to help with the insurance-to-value mandate for their specific properties, it is not likely that regulators will endorse efforts by insurers to shift the burden of establishing insurance adequacy totally to their customers.

The Value of Book of Business Management Programs

Today, there are very important reasons for insurers to continue expanding their ITV business initiatives to also include a comprehensive review and updating process for property business on the books by adopting what is described herein as a sustainable book of business management program. The dynamic nature of property business described earlier suggests why insurance providers and their agents should consider implementing a systematic book of business review program, beginning with updating of legacy business, archiving the data, and reviewing it on a regular basis with the people who know homes the best—*the owners.*

As mentioned previously, because insurance companies have already adopted the proven total component approach and technology for their new business process it is therefore logical to assume the viability of expanding their ITV process to their legacy books of property business in order to address deficiencies and better serve clients, especially when large numbers of policies may not have been reviewed for decades. As discussed later, the opportunity to bring legacy business into the insurance to value process is simple to initiate and monitor, using analytical methods to identify suspect accounts and direct consumer contact techniques to update accounts. Given that the undervaluation issue has been front and center in the press for the past several years, the added benefits are certainly financial but also offer regulatory relief and a public support perspective.

The Legacy Book—A Valued Asset

A very relevant consideration for starting a book of business management program is maintaining the value of the book itself in today's challenging economic landscape. On average, less than 15 percent of net premiums earned come from new insurance policies; the vast majority of revenues are earned from recurring business. Finding, selling, and managing new insurance transactions, while on everyone's mind, have a long payback cycle that provides only limited contribution to earnings the first year a policy is written. It is estimated that the cost to acquire new homeowners insurance accounts far outweighs profits achieved in year one, actually requiring two or more years to catch up or reimburse.

By comparison, existing homeowners business renewing year after year makes a substantial contribution to bottom line results when properly valued and priced, requires minimal support or handling, and generally can be counted on to renew for a minimum of eight years. This strongly suggests that proactive strategies such as recalculating coverage limits at time of renewal through continuous book of business review would have profound and very positive additive effects on long term business viability.

When concerns over coverage adequacy become a recurring theme in the underwriting process, operating ratios rise, the company's competitive position deteriorates, and overall ratings suffer.

Attention to a company's largest single asset, its book of business, strengthens the carrier's overall financial position. Also, valuation improvements have a cumulative impact over the lifetime that policies are maintained, especially when other rate adjustments occur, which is why investment in ongoing book of business management should not be considered a one-time event. Rather, it is an investment that pays dividends for years. In addition, because coverage becomes the focal point of renewing business when disasters occur, consumer loyalty and overall retention rates are protected when companies develop a sustainable book of business management strategy. At the same time, the need for regulatory oversight is seen to decline.

When the industry and others become focused on enduring under insurance challenges , especially following natural disasters, the response is too often dominated by emphasis on the next policy written, even when the book of business itself can present the largest opportunity for change. This is especially true when limited or no building characteristic or other underwriting information is maintained or updated. Gathering home characteristics using modern component-based valuation technology and thereafter archiving and recalculating values are the missing ingredients in the overall insurance-to-value issue.

MSB has performed numerous analytics studies on books of homeowners business in order to better compare and understand variances that occur over time between managing the book through a *best practices* approach and simply indexing business through use of a generic indexing factor. As described later in this chapter, gaps often occur between indexed coverage and the realities of a dynamic book of property business. These gaps can quickly build to a 20 percent or greater variance in coverage over as few as ten years between indexed insurable values and values that better reflect the exact property characteristics, irrespective of inflationary changes in labor and material costs.

Increased Customer Interest

Given the lengthy payback period for new business, retaining existing business is a top priority for insurers. Retention, investment and reinvestment, cross-selling, and up-selling are all enhanced by improvements insurers make to their existing books of business. In light of the attention on coverage limits expressed from a variety of media, consumer, and regulatory outlets over the past three years, particular attention to initiatives surrounding building valuations are seen as net positives by policyholders.

For example, in a 2005 study of customer satisfaction and retention, marketing information firm J.D. Power and Associates reported that insurance carriers whose customers understood their insurance providers were actively reviewing their policy needs reported high levels of increased loyalty and enjoyed an advantage of sustained renewal rates, referral rates, and upside growth potential. This occurred regardless of price. These same customers were also deemed less likely to shop their business and were more than amenable to help the insurance company with its business management process. Further, the study reported that:

- Defections are triggered by poor service—not price.

- Satisfied customers are more likely to say they will recommend and subsequently do recommend more often.

- Satisfied customers are far less likely to respond to competitive price offers.

- The majority of customers rating their carrier a "10" would not consider switching just to save money.

At the same time, the J.D. Power study also found that:

- The majority of policyholders report they have not been approached to recalculate replacement cost values in more than five years.

- Homeowners are making significant structural improvements in their homes.

- One-third of homeowners making said improvements failed to notify their carriers.

- A majority of policyholders hold their carrier or agent responsible for estimating replacement cost.

Insurance consumers appreciate attention to their insurance needs.

Despite the fact that insureds hold agents and carriers responsible, experts express concern that too little attention has been placed on the valuable asset of the existing book of business, failing to capitalize on long term earnings opportunities inherent in it. When property business is simply indexed year after year in an effort to maintain coverage adequacy, blind spots occur. However, these can easily be avoided using today's technology and services for archiving, analytics, and updating.

Additional Reasons for Sustained Book of Business Management

The legacy book is the insurance company's largest single asset, a reliable source of income with an average renewal rate of 85 percent per year, generating income for operations as well as future investment. For these reasons, the introduction of modern book of business review, updating, and archiving strategies as a minimal innovation has great merit financially. In addition, a book of business management program:

·   Adds meaningful data

·   Improves positive visibility in the marketplace

·   Defines market position and advantage

·   Identifies opportunities for greater profitability

·   Uncovers misaligned rating territories, now estimated at 15 percent of a legacy book

·   Analyzes hazard exposures

·   Stays current with changes due to home remodeling, now estimated at 6 percent of a book per year

·   Enhances corporate brand

The Analytics Component

In Chapter 7, the added value of archiving data collected about policies written was advanced and underscored. It is nowhere more important to have detailed inside and outside building characteristics and other risk specific data available for review than in managing books of property business. Not only is the individual carrier's book relevant, but an industry-level database gives individual carriers insights into which property records are most likely best performers and which ones likely need attention. As a first step in developing a book of business management program as well as adopting the *best practices* mandate, isolating those records that are likely to be undervalued, as well as updating and converting records that have limited information to the modern component approach, is made easier through use of modern analytics insights applied to the property book.

The analytics model as applied to a modern book of business management program is a scientific method of comparing and contrasting individual policies found in books of property business with comparable records either inside an insurer's archived data files or inside an overall industry database. Industry norms as well as better performance criteria are used to measure such things as coverage viability, suspected under insurance, adequacy of building characteristics input used to calculate home replacement costs, exposures to naturally occurring hazards, and much more. When applied specifically to managing coverage adequacy in a book of property business, especially when the book has not been reviewed for some period of time (more often than not decades), book of business analytics provide a reference point or benchmark for carriers to thoroughly understand their books both before and after strategies suggested by analytics are applied. These reference points allow carriers with even minimal information about home characteristics and features, or even with no information at all, to identify specific risks that need updating, the extent of information required for each policy record, and the anticipated amount of under valuation likely to occur. While insurers can align to their own records, having access to a comprehensive industry database, such as MSB's archive of nearly 30 million property records, provides another statistically meaningful layer or comparison point from which to isolate those problem accounts that require prompt action. (See Figure 8.1.)

Figure 8.1

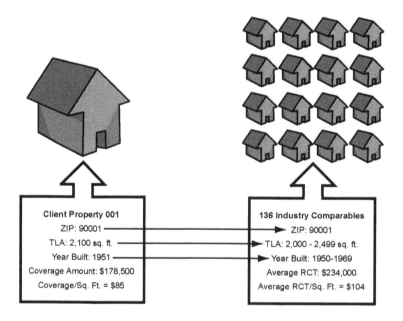

Client Property 001
ZIP: 90001
TLA: 2,100 sq. ft.
Year Built: 1951
Coverage Amount: $178,500
Coverage/Sq. Ft. = $85

136 Industry Comparables
ZIP: 90001
TLA: 2,000 - 2,499 sq. ft.
Year Built: 1950-1969
Average RCT: $234,000
Average RCT/Sq. Ft. = $104

Matching one insured property or complete books of business against comprehensive industry databases provides another statistically meaningful layer or comparison point from which to isolate problem accounts that require prompt underwriting action. Here, the cost-per-square-foot comparison is a benchmark against how the industry as a whole is valuating similar homes.

Even those individual problem accounts with little or no data currently on file can be isolated and ameliorated. For example, through a unique combination of analytics modeling, industry-wide property data, and current public record data, MSB identifies profiles likely to fit the property address. Using this basic profile of home characteristics, a summary replacement cost value can be determined and used to measure against current Coverage A and the benchmark industry coverage for similar homes in particular ZIP codes, rating territories, or economic zones. Coverage differences are isolated and referred for action steps, depending upon the degree of variance identified between current coverage limits and what the newly created valuation record displays. Thereafter, the home characteristic assumptions made by this process can be documented and confirmed through policyholder contact. Then a final insurable value update can be added to the underwriting file. Thereafter, insurers are able to use the new record as the source for ongoing book of business management.

Figure 8.2

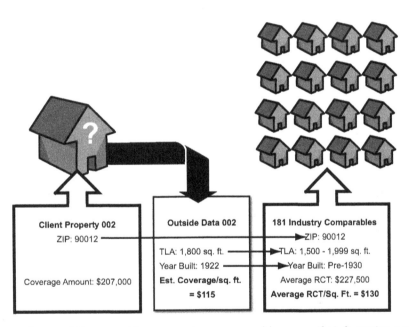

Even when property characteristics are not known, carriers can use address-specific information now available from a variety of information sources outside the insurance forum to evaluate and trend property business. Here, the carrier's record, which included only address, ZIP code, and coverage amount, was augmented by building characteristics from other reliable outside sources.

Analytics insights are helpful for managing books of property business in a number of situations. Consider a property writer with a book of business that has significant numbers of vintage or older homes that never utilized component estimating with the capability to accommodate homes built using designs and construction methods no longer in common use today; or a carrier that has business in new emerging markets segments with code or soft cost impact that has not been updated at the local level; or an insurer that has business heavily influenced by upscale homes or extensive remodeling. In each of these instances, the possibility of an indexing-only updating program being sufficient to maintain profitable business and add to a company's growth position is unlikely to occur.

However, insurers should consider that the analytics model helps to further define typical home construction in specified market segments, with even address-specific information now available from a variety of information sources outside the insurance forum. The model generates representative home characteristics files that find blind spots in coverage or can be used to streamline books of business conversions to component-based valuation methods in a quicker, less expensive, simpler, and less invasive process. Analytics models provide the first level of the management process for working more effectively with legacy business, which has been identified as the remaining problem area in what remains of the under valuation issue facing both the U.S. economy and Canada.

Developing and successfully implementing strategies that maximize the return on existing business, including reunderwriting the property book to produce *risk-specific* insights that better define business at hand and then archiving data to be able to stay current, has been shown to generate immediate financial returns of up to five times the investment made. And, as stated previously, these types of revaluation programs, in which values are either increased or decreased, are welcomed today by consumers and regulators alike who witnessed the catastrophic events of 2003 through 2005 and appreciate the value-added relevance of proactive approaches to property business. In fact, examining the past five years of book of business updating programs MSB has managed (especially MSB *direct contact ITV* services) shows that retention is either unchanged or actually improves when insurers, agents, and their customers collaborate positively on insurance-to-value initiatives in order to update coverage.

That remodeling expenditures accounted for 40 percent of all residential construction and more than 2 percent of the U.S. economy[1], according to the Joint Center for Housing Studies of Harvard University, suggests it is literally a requirement for insurers to make book business maintenance a new priority.

The Case for Obsolescing Indexing

As mentioned previously, many insurers have relied on three-digit adjustment factors or an inflationary trend index multiplier to update coverage limits. For instance, a 3 percent inflationary increase in the items of labor and material would be represented as a 1.03 index multiplier an insurer might apply to policies in certain geographical areas at time of renewal. Insurers could apply this single factor to each risk as it renewed, thereby incorporating the trending for common cost concerns in the coverage limit for each renewal.

While some adjustment is better than none at all, indexing assumes the book of business is static, which is hardly the case. In fact, book characteristics change annually, and inflation affects different homes differently. The average remodeling project costs $10,000, and 6 percent of homes are now affected by remodeling. Indexing does nothing to uncover or correct errors in the initial ITV calculation or address underwriting questions as policies renew.

Additionally, changing housing trends (including the addition of more complex *mixed construction*) and the emergence of more tightly focused economic segments with their own cost variable concerns has a numbing effect over time on business that is managed through index factors derived from industry averages in broad geographic segments in what were once homogenous areas. Ultimately, this reduces precision and long term profitability.

As illustrated by Figure 8.3, relying on indexing leaves policyholders with potentially undervalued homes and carriers with premiums that are not commensurate with risk.

Figure 8.3

Improved Renewal Calculation			
Indexing Only		**Record Maintenance Program**	
Current Coverage A Limit	$100,000	Current Coverage A Limit	$100,000
Local Index Factor	x 1.03	Remodeling Impact	+ $10,000
New Coverage A Limit	$103,000	True Renewal Base	$110,000
Additional Annual Premium*	$12.00	True Component Recalulation	1.07
		New Coverage A Limit	$107,700
		True Additional Annual Premium*	$70.80
		Premium Advantage	$58.80

* Assuming a rate of $4.00 per $100

This chart illustrates the coverage and premium impact that can occur if carriers simply index property books year after year. Indexing does not uncover home changes or upgrades, leaving customers with potentially undervalued homes and carriers with premiums that are not commensurate with exposures assumed.

Clearly, managing business throughout its lifecycle by using a strategy that incorporates comprehensive characteristics data provides a significant advantage.

Additionally, much of this management can be automated by simply reprocessing characteristic data through the component-based calculation engine at the time of policy renewal to generate an updated replacement cost, essentially replacing the earlier index-only calculation. Furthermore, by having access to archived data, the carrier or agent can produce simple mailers or other material to present the information currently on file to the policyholder for review and updating. If building characteristics do change, the policy record can be updated and then reprocessed through the valuation system. Companies like MSB can manage these programs for companies so that the updated data can be verified by a competent third party and reprocessed, eliminating the need to retain more expensive appraisal services.

This type of active book management also demonstrates an expertise on the part of the insurer that can be a point of competitive differentiation in the marketplace. For instance, particularly in today's comparative-quoting environment, knowledgeable consumers may question large differences between quotes and choose the carrier that demonstrates the more sophisticated valuation method. Also, as the aforementioned J.D. Power & Associates study revealed, when coverage updates are actually based on critical review of home characteristics between insurer and policyholder, customer loyalty increases.

In the following graphs, actual archived building characteristics data is used to analyze the make-up of a book of property business. As discussed in the Chapter 6 discussion about emerging markets, many insurers are often amazed to learn that when data is actually collected and analyzed the profile of their homeowners business in specific geographies is not as expected.

Figure 8.4

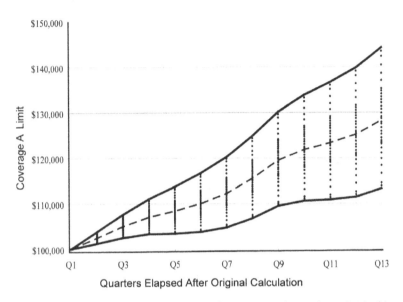

Indexing Impact Analysis

This graph illustrates the dramatic deviation, over time, of Coverage A limits for individual homes developed from indexing versus recalculated replacement cost values. For this study, all properties were normalized to $100,000 at Q1 to better demonstrate this effect. Note that the individual data points of recalculated limits for actual homes in the book (located within solid lines indicating extreme records) vary greatly from the average of the index (broken line).

Through use of today's book of business management techniques, including the collection and archiving of risk-specific data, detailed analysis is possible, leading to complete understanding of what a book of business looks like and whether it requires remediation. Collection of home characteristics data at an industry-wide level offers the potential for comparisons at the aggregate level between a particular homeowners book and the industry at large, as shown in Figures 8.5 and 8.6.

Figure 8.5

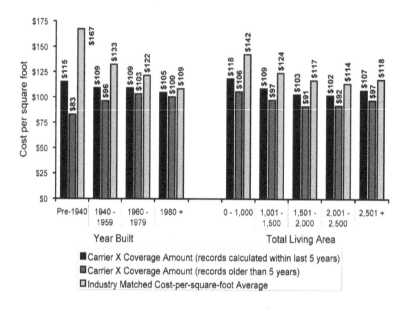

Book Profile Comparison at the Industry Level

In this example, a cost-per-square-foot comparison of the carrier versus the industry reveals that coverage is below the industry, more noticeably for older and smaller properties, and especially for valuation records generated more than 5 years ago. Addressing this disparity can lead to coverage, pricing, marketing, and risk selection improvements over time.

Regardless of whether the movement to book of business management is a requirement of state regulators or has been instituted by the insurer as an important and effective protective measure for policyholders and insurers alike, a movement toward a book-of-business management program that incorporates best practices has begun. The program outlined herein offers more opportunity to establish and maintain the most adequate coverage and, at the same time, generates premiums that are commensurate and defendable for each risk insured. The program also lowers loss and operating ratios, mitigates the need to perform large book-of-business revaluation programs every few years, reduces reinsurance rates and errors and omissions exposures, and ultimately creates better public policy.

Book of Business Management Steps

That books of property business are critical to the insurers' long-term viability continues to underscore the need to put the existing book at center stage. As we have discussed, performing book of business management should be an integral part of the renewal business process. Just as important, book of business management should be used to express knowledge of the base of business once archived and to offer underwriters and actuaries critical insights that were unable to be discerned in the past. For example, management strategies involving insights from book of business analytics can help ensure that profitable business is maintained going forward through the use of various scorecards that identify inconsistencies in how property business is written, underwriters or agents who are responsible for good business practices or who need more training, and whether the business underwritten each day meets the overall company profile. Once the analytics process is engaged, these other book of business management steps can be employed:

- Collect risk-specific information in a component approach for every new home insured

- Identify existing business that requires conversion and/or updating (see Figure 8.6)

- Compare home characteristics of existing policies with new profiles designed from carriers' existing or other files

- Perform verification, augmentation, and correction of new home profiles with policyholders by the carrier, its agents, or competent third parties

- Update coverage limits using the final home characteristics profile

- Append hazard or other geospatial information into policy records

- Archive all information collected

- Share archived information with policyholders on a regular basis

- Reprocess each record on renewal using the same estimating tools used to write new business, prudently replacing inadequate indexing processes

Figure 8.6

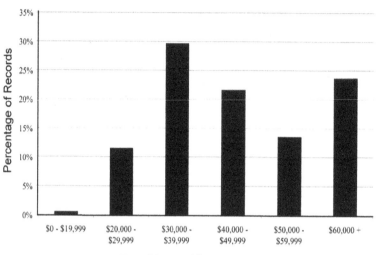

Assumed Component Cost Analysis

In this example, the carrier analyzed over 100,000 policy records to target the book segments that most needed reconstruction cost review. The analysis compares the variances between current Coverage A and reconstruction cost calculated by component-based methods including construction assumptions made by knowledge tables. The carrier decided to target those records, nearly 25 percent of the book, where assumed components exceeded $60,000.

Engaging in a book of business management process like the one described previously helps carriers eliminate the need for mass re-underwriting projects, which are not only time-intensive but unpopular with agents and policyholders. Additionally, carriers can review large numbers of risks easily and automatically, replacing outdated valuation methods utilized within the book, uncovering hazard and underwriting exposures by involving the homeowner, and correcting other errors such as territory alignment. All these benefits lead to the further advantage of collecting adequate premium for risks insured. Equally important, better book of business management enables carriers to comply with regulatory directives and even stay ahead of regulatory demands and customer expectations.

Organizational Strategies: The Impact of Nonconstruction Data

This book has dedicated considerable space to defining and proving the advantages and impact of modern methods of valuing buildings. However, in order to fully maximize these advantages, risk assessment for individual properties *must no longer be limited to evaluating the structure itself.* Instead, because property risk and desirability for insurance protection are influenced by many more variables today than simply construction cost, other considerations such as the site the structure rests on and the surrounding neighborhood are now entering the modern insurance to value equation.

Studies performed by the industry over the past five years revealed that the entire setting for property risks presented exposures that could not only be delineated and understood, but also used in modeling risk desirability and even pricing property business. Technology is once again an important contributor to this understanding. Modern geocoding and mapping techniques of site-specific data can be used, since these settings are either proximate to or literally underneath properties being insured, resulting in a major refinement to the overall insurance to value process.

In fact, such information as proximity to brush fire hazards, sinkholes, bodies of water, coastal zones impacted by hurricanes, or earthquake zones is a relevant part of the overall concern of insuring to value. Knowledge of susceptibility to brushfire damage, available fire protection, wind or hail zone exposures, territory alignment, and other issues surrounding the positioning of risks in their environment can now be presented electronically when building property estimating is performed, refining the overall view of the total property risk profile as well as impacting risk selection and pricing.

Updating the insurance to value equation to also include a holistic view of the building and its setting provides added benefits to carriers, because risks that are highly susceptible to major hazard exposures tend to have very high combined ratios that can be mitigated if understood. From a premium as well as risk desirability perspective, insurance to value determinations that also include hazard summaries for the location and the real property are not only possible to achieve but recommended. Following this reasoning, the original formula for establishing premium, represented as

Replacement cost x Rate = Premium, would now become

Replacement Cost (Building + Hazard) x Rate = Risk-specific Premium.

Research performed by MSB over the past three years has determined that insurers that are incorporating broader site-based considerations as part of their insurance to value initiatives reliably identified the 2 percent of risks that produce as much as 200 percent combined ratios. Further, the research established that mapping techniques employed when reviewing existing books of property business revealed territory misalignments in as many as 15 percent of the property records studied, generating concern over risk desirability, pricing, and compliance.

The utilization of modern, Web-based platforms for calculating total component estimates also enables insurers to capture and display site-specific hazards, building a more complete profile of the risk than ever before. This information is also stored for future review, building what MSB calls the risk profile record. These same Web-based hosting platforms are also invaluable for use in connection with any number of decisioning technologies at the disposal of carriers today that automate cumbersome or repetitive actions performed by underwriters and agents.

For example, decisioning technologies access various risk-specific hazard or other databases as necessary based on such indicators as age of dwelling, ZIP code, value, or company underwriting preferences. These tools, built underneath the insuring to value application on a Web-hosted platform, automatically enact rules insurers have created in their businesses for each situation, such as guidelines related to on-site or surrounding hazards or thresholds of property value that require manual underwriting review. Once rules are automated in the overall insuring to value model, they help companies and their agents support the underwriting effort with automated *approve, decline,* or *refer* decisions, place risks into specific rating categories or tiers, refer accounts for ordering/obtaining inspections, ask for and apply the data from credit or loss history reports, or route applications for policy issuance. Blending all of the relevant information surrounding an insured site now completes this broader definition of modern insurance to value and can be applied interactively risk by risk when business is first written or globally in batch mode for updating existing accounts. Incorporating this broader definition of ITV within a carrier's approve/decline decisioning process also reveals previously unseen problems and generates better risk assessment, underwriting, and pricing. This more rounded approach ensures premium adequacy and regulatory compliance, placing business on the books that is better understood, predictable, and aligned with the carrier's business model.

This comprehensive approach, however, is still in its infancy, similar in some respects to where the introduction of total-component estimating was in the 1990s. Even so, early results demonstrate viability and likelihood for success. MSB research, coupled with lessons learned since 1996 demonstrate that a proactive book-of-business management program can have an even greater impact than reengineering the rating process.

Needed Actions

Results achieved over the past ten years demonstrate real progress on multiple fronts encouraging building cost vendors to align more closely with their insurance clients in the vital area of coverage adequacy and book of business management. As described, concentrating solely on new business does not address an insurer's long-term business needs when it comes to the topic of insuring to value.

Opportunities created by better book management are also broader than the impact on any one carrier. When MSB publishes the ITV Quality Index for the industry each year, announcing the estimated amount of improvement occurring on the valuation front, the largest component that moves the Quality Index positively continues to be the work insurers have done converting legacy business still on the books to current valuation methodologies. When the 75 percent of property business that was undervalued by 35 percent improved to 58 percent undervalued by 21 percent, the result was that more than $8 billion in lost revenues was received each year. Considering the relative size of legacy books still in force, the overall financial structure of property business improves dramatically as well by better book management. Certainly more needs to be done, but the industry is on the right path.

And encouragingly, the time has never been better for the industry to take this path. Advances in technology, especially database management, make the type of book of business management this book has illustrated not only possible, but increasingly practical. The vendor community has also developed increasingly powerful and ubiquitous data-driven solutions, helping to spread the cost of development over a large base and ultimately driving down the cost of both system acquisition and data access for carriers and agents.

By applying the techniques described in this book across an entire book of legacy business, insurers stay a step ahead of regulatory mandates that are increasingly likely due to the resurgence of large numbers of catastrophic losses and the degree of operational sophistication now available. They improve their results and discover new market opportunities. And ultimately, they fulfill their most important mission: protecting the financial interests of the homeowners they insure.

1   R05-1: The Changing Structure of the Home Remodeling Industry, Joint Centers for Housing Studies at Harvard

Chapter 9

Modern Insurance to Value Enhancements

As important as other enhancements have been in the area of modern, ITV solutions, the remarkable innovations that occurred over the last fifteen years in computer technology and the associated use of sophisticated databases have propelled the business forward at a rapid pace, especially since 1999 when the market began to realize the potential of the World Wide Web. Today's breed of system is not only a logic-driven calculation engine that sorts input and then selects just those components of construction necessary to replace homes on a risk specific basis. It also provides a service-oriented program that connects all of the constituents of the insuring process from policyholders, to agents, to underwriters, to claims adjusters, and any other parties privy to the information. From this perspective, today's modern ITV systems are a *medium of exchange* for collecting and archiving data that will be continuously referenced in ongoing policy management strategies through much needed communication continuously occurring between policyholders and insurance professionals. Even when regulators are involved, the systems provide a frame of reference for policy management and coverage.

With the introduction of Web-hosted technologies, the need for costly investments maintaining in-house estimating systems (with associated updating and distribution) shifted from carriers and agents to system providers who were able to spread development costs across all of their users, giving significantly more capability and functionality based on the investment of the collective, thereby generating vast savings to individual users. The Web also provides greater overall scalability and instant system updates because the management of the programs occurs behind the scenes in the vendor site, relieving users of this responsibility.

Software solutions that have emerged from most third-party suppliers further introduce the ability to wrap around, plug into, or otherwise connect with legacy management systems in ways that are not invasive, eliminating disruptions of the legacy environment through expensive and time-consuming custom programming projects. Modern Web-enabled valuation solutions combine advances in database management and storage, geocoding and geospatial techniques, hazard databases, credit, loss history, data decisioning, and many more necessary programs to easily enable insurers to write and maintain property business instantly within a single program. MSB has identified this concept as the Hub Strategy for property writers because it enables them to connect all of the needed risk assessment pieces of the policy issuance and updating process through one point, the ITV technology hosted on a Web-enabled platform. A representative model for this advance is shown in Figure 9.1 below.

Modern Underwriting "Hub" Solution

Figure 9.1

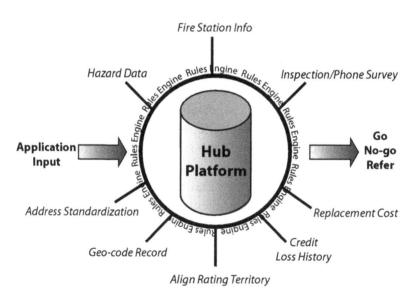

Modern Web-hosted valuation technologies serve as a hub, connecting all needed risk assessment pieces of the policy issuance and updating process, including automated decision-making, through one point.

In particular, these systems give users increased flexibility to:

- Develop their own direct-to-consumer and/or totally Web-enabled business solutions.

- Access a ready-made, turnkey platform to collect relevant information from every side of the insuring process simultaneously and place it in a virtually limitless central storage facility.

- Incorporate any third-party database or service provider as needed in the insuring process.

·   Link all sides of the sales distribution channel in a single hub platform that gives identity to each, yet provides a general overview to the insurer.

·   Develop full analytics insights into any phase of the insuring process.

·   Create scorecards on sales channel performance with specific insights as to whether or not each sales channel is developing the specific risk profile intended when carriers offer insurance service.

This last point is one worth considering more closely. Because ITV systems are now repositories for vast amounts of risk-specific information in totally protected and secure environments accessible to just those users involved in the insuring process, the database or *record* that emerges for the first time gives a clear and concise picture that is able to be interrogated to determine what kind of property business is insured. In analytics studies performed by MSB over the past three years, it has been interesting to note the reactions of some insurers when they learned that the kind of property risks they intended to write through specific channels were often totally different in the end. Before the evolution of the Hub Strategy, there was no easy method of collecting and accessing salient details of risks in a manner that could be easily studied. Now, should irregularities be found in the book of business profile, remedial action can be taken because specifics driving events are accessible.

With technology mechanisms in place to support the next generation of property business management strategies, best practices, and analytics oversight, the task remains for the industry to complete its effort to integrate the policy management and ITV process in a way that incorporates current automated workflows for the new business and renewal processes. In the past, ITV systems tended to be stand-alone programs, isolated from the underwriting workflow on personal computers, paper manuals, and brochures, or, if installed internally, limited to generating a single-number, providing little or no useful information that was retrievable. Today, the possibility exists to create a detailed history for each risk, inclusive of all of the changes and iterations that occur in the sales and underwriting process. This is literally the archived record for each risk that becomes the key for insightful analysis of the profitable books of business. And, as discussed in Chapter 8, Book of Business Management is the next frontier for insurance to value.

This technology strategy is not a distant prophecy. Through a combination of methods described in this book—archiving data , managing risk assessment strategies, analytics, creating multi-tiered and more effective pricing models, and developing new policies and coverages reflective of narrowly defined market segments emerging in the economy—this next generation risk management is possible today. By adhering to *best practices*, adopting modern book of business management in part to provide access to vast amounts of data unavailable before, blending detailed component-level input and calculation results with other, non-constructive factors as described in Chapter 8 (such as hazard, fire protection, location, age, and loss experience), and leveraging new levels of decision technology, insurers can attain a remarkable competitive advantage.

The Construction Variable

For proof that this vision is possible today, look to the automobile insurance industry. Automobile insurers have shown great sophistication in being able to use modern book-of-business management and risk modeling strategies to better understand, select, and price vehicles and drivers with pinpoint accuracy specific to the conditions found. The same type of analytic research used to understand auto insurance will ultimately become essential programs of property writers and is, in fact, already occurring at proactive insurance companies. Today, when so much data can be collected and effectively managed through data repositories, the next step in the development of insurance to value is rolling up the claims and underwriting results with insights from construction professionals to build new kinds of *risk-based modeling* solutions for the property insurance industry.

The risk-based modeling program combines building characteristics with loss experience to present a scientifically-derived exposure summary or score. As a result, the summary is based on what a property risk looks like in connection with not only an insurer's own claims and underwriting experience for this same kind of risk positioned geographically, by age, and by specifically defined features, but also in comparison with the industry and economy at large. As important as the traditional variables of underwriting and claim experience are, however, one other is extremely important in order to get this process right: the inclusion of third-party construction knowledge including construction-related trends affecting residential construction virtually everywhere in the economy.

In the property insurance arena, risk-based modeling is a promising use of archived data, trends analysis, and emerging analytics techniques first tried when MSB was studying archived property records coming from Web-based ITV input storage. Because insurance carriers are now able to collect and manage account-specific information, blending these factors, especially home characteristics and claims results with details of local construction trends, begins to predict risk desirability trends. It is important to note that these are construction-specific criteria and, therefore, very objective. The resulting models can become an adjunct or substitute for other risk selection criteria such as credit.

To be successful, insurers must have access to industry-wide construction trends from which to compare results and formulate strategies. The reason is that over time, construction advantages as well as flaws have occurred that add insights as to why certain peril-specific loss patterns occur. These can include everything from code changes to obsolescence to substitutions of less available items. By blending these variables, companies will be in a new position to develop property-specific scores for individual perils, leading to insights on risk selection, more competitive pricing, and underwriting models predicated on the likelihood of a property to react positively or negatively to particular insured events. Therefore, the databases emerging from the modern insurance-to-value initiatives offer the opportunity to develop trends analysis reflective of a peril-specific view of underwriting and pricing driven by construction characteristics. The models used to analyze this information are not simple but are expected to automate modern scoring engines. From this perspective, a partnership between ITV providers with strong construction insights and the insurance industry will emerge at even higher levels because the construction expertise that is needed generally comes from these third-party professionals. Also, because large industry databases are also emerging through these third parties on both the underwriting and claims side, the need to create greater alliances beyond simple estimating solutions will evolve.

The Total Industry View

Figure 9.2

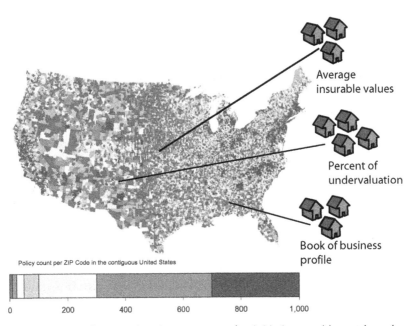

Extensive databases emerging from modern insurance-to-value initiatives enable trends analyses and insights reflective of a total industry view for a vast number of information points, such as average insurable values, percentage of undervaluation, etc., allowing each individual carrier's book of business to be analyzed in comparison to the industry as a whole.

To achieve *risk-based modeling predictive solutions* faster, analysts will ultimately align the characteristics of already bound risks with ideal business candidates, incorporating claims experience in the confirmation process, in order to develop tiers of opportunity, pricing metrics for each tier, and special conditions that ultimately filter into insurance contracts. However, the missing ingredient we identified previously can be referred to as the *construction variable*.

When it comes to property business, a deep understanding of what drives loss experience from the construction perspective is essential. While carrier information can be segmented by locality, age of construction, style, and other characteristics, risk-based models must be supplemented with input from construction experts such as MSB or the Institute for Building and Home Safety that report on structural flaws and/or improvements. These construction experts are able to report, particularly by age and location, design flaws that have occurred over time, affecting specific home profiles that could be expected to increase loss frequency and severity arising out of certain perils.

An example recently studied by MSB and discussed in Chapter 7 involved analysis of hail losses in a sector of homes built in the 1980s. As mentioned earlier, MSB identified that homes of that era built with vinyl siding had a significantly higher frequency of hail losses than vinyl-sided homes built in other decades. More importantly with respect to risk-based modeling, MSB was also able to identify *why the higher frequency occurred.* In this example, siding was not consistently supported by sheathing and underlayment, which resulted in high susceptibility to loss from the specified perils of hail. Therefore, the increased susceptibility to this type of loss in homes of this vintage could lead modelers to conclude that writing risks with this characteristics profile would adversely impact the underwriting processes for the hail peril. In turn, this might lead to a peril-based scoring process that would ultimately influence the risk assessment process, the alignment of specified risks in new tiering models, and/or the pricing sophistication developed from a fact-based system. Additional "go/no-go" strategies might emerge based on a carrier's appetite for a susceptibility to loss score, or other policy conditions could be created.

Once designed, this kind of model can be automated as part of a larger risk analysis and selection process using the construction characteristics gathered when the component-based estimate of insurable value is performed or updated. Overlaid with construction-specific rules, this model becomes an *indicator of risk desirability* that can be measured and priced accordingly. The evolution of archiving of component-level input made this possible; therefore, insurers concerned with adoption of more sophisticated risk-based modeling strategies are at a disadvantage if they do not invest in modern component-based insurance-to-value solutions.

Every bit of data gathered in a modern component-based valuation tool is a rich resource for analytics and, ultimately, risk-based modeling, which is a further incentive for fully utilizing the data collection attributes of these tools to gather as much interior and exterior building characteristic information at the point of sale and as part of the ongoing book of business management strategy. (Refer to Appendix 2). From there, insurers have insights they will use to develop risk tolerance levels that align with new pricing tiers based on varying degrees of tolerance. If an insurer is also collecting additional property, occupant, or location-specific data, this data can be incorporated in the study to improve predictive results. This data could include number and type of residents, income, credit, and more. This additional data can be tested for predictability before being incorporated into the model.

Analytics Input

The factors that contribute to one cause of loss do not necessarily factor into the likelihood of another; as a matter of fact, at times they are quite unrelated. Studying different loss causes separately enables better understanding of overall loss experience. It is easier to reconcile study results with real-life experience by focusing on one peril type at a time rather than to aggregate all experiences once the data is available to break things into these salient parts. The insurance contract is often viewed as a global resource when disaster hits, and, as a result, many insurance companies still treat their pricing models globally or as a single tier for all risk events. However, using modern database resources aligned with third-party expertise and data analytics regarding loss, construction and age, home characteristics, and more, make it possible if not beneficial to generate peril-specific outlooks that can stand on their own or be merged as a composite view since the underlying assumptions are so factually based.

The work being done today to design new levels of risk assessment models incorporates sophisticated risk selection criteria and associated competitive pricing schedules with correlations derived. It ultimately leads to marketing criteria that better predict loss. This is of increasing interest inside the carrier's own actuarial department, where staff examining these issues often works in association with qualified third parties. The process then breaks down the replacement cost side of the *premium determination formula* in order to use new kinds of modeling to correlate the input from replacement cost estimating with experience modeling or risk-based pricing. The purpose is to better establish the ramifications of multiple total component estimating building characteristics on overall risk desirability, including:

- likelihood of loss versus specific building characteristics,

- desirability of risk for individual covered perils,

· pricing adequacy for individual covered perils, and

· market positioning.

In itself, this work is becoming a new science inside the arena of insurance to value, often referred to as *determination analytics,* making insurance to value even more important in the property insuring process from a perspective usually not considered with this work process—*actuarial studies.*

For the first time, now that data repositories are raising a vast amount of information for consideration, actuarial analytics can be designed to separate archived data by cause of loss into different variables for use in more sophisticated ways. Roof type, for example, may become an important actuarial component of the rating as well as risk assessment model, especially if roof type is determined to impact fire claims in a particular location or era of construction; similarly, piping of a certain kind mixed with age of construction in another area can be a predictor of water losses. Therefore, interjecting *determination analytics* processes that can actually be codified and automated across a wide mix of covered property perils and building types, especially when policies are written, will enhance the predictive ability of the underwriting process, and for forward-looking insurance providers, make them more competitive. This will become an even more effective business strategy when insurance providers are able to grow premiums while reducing loss frequency, enhancing margins and leading to better rating formulas for properties that score better on overall peril-by-peril summaries.

Conclusion

After insurance companies initiated the strategies set forth in the first edition of *Insuring to Value,* operating ratios of 125 percent and more in the homeowners line gave way to years with ratios in the low 100s and lower. While insurers took many steps to achieve this improvement, including refining policy language, eliminating certain coverage concerns, and taking premium adjustments, it is clear that the problem of undervaluation improved by more than 25 percent since that first edition, while lost premium of more than $8 billion has been recovered as a direct result of increased values. At the same time, new technologies emerged in the property insurance arena, creating an impact that will continue to be felt positively for years to come and helping insurers gain new insights through the proposed insurance to value model that will change how property business is written and priced.

In order for these trends to persist, the industry must continue to work toward utilizing precise reconstruction cost data to not only estimate coverage and establish accurate replacement costs in the underwriting process, but, just as critically, to protect their customers and reduce claims severity. Many other profound benefits will be realized from archiving and sharing data, embracing a broader definition of insuring to value, and ultimately using insurance to value as the centerpiece for modern analytics strategies. In order for property business to realize its potential in these areas, new and expanded use of book-of-business management programs will be particularly important. It will no longer be sufficient to simply index property records if insurers want to have leading-edge analytics capability and competitive advantage; they will need to manage with their data providers, an ongoing book-of-business review process that continuously refreshes their policy-record database. This can then be aligned with risk desirability models that go far beyond ordinary renewal business programs. Furthermore, this insight will provide additional competitive advantages. It is recommended by the regulators and rating bureaus as well. It is a win/win situation for all involved.

The successful development of risk-based modeling lies with companies that have industry-wide property characteristics and claims databases available as well as the Internet technology and analytics expertise to bring the vision of this modeling to fruition. In the next ten years, not only will insurance to value evolve to include the foundational concepts presented in earlier chapters, but it will be instrumental in formulating new levels of risk assessment and pricing sophistication. These new levels will enable underwriters to pinpoint risk assessment to specific perils or causes, ensuring increased competitive advantage, profitability, customer satisfaction, and security and sustainability for this too often fragile industry.

However, before these benefits can be realized, insurance carriers will have to finish converting legacy square-foot or inaccessible valuation data in books of business to a modern component-based format. Even though 90 percent of insurers today use a component-based approach, the preponderance of legacy business on the books has not been converted to the component-based approach. This means that today millions of home insurance risks are still locked in the earlier square-foot process with the associated potential inaccuracies. Once all books of business are converted, remaining shortfalls in coverage adequacy, with associated lost premium dollars estimated to be another $8 billion, will be overcome.

Fortunately, both the methods and the technology have emerged that will allow insurers to reap these benefits. Now it is up to the industry to respond.

GLOSSARY

Actual cash value (ACV) is a method for placing value on property as of the time of its loss or damage. ACV may be determined as replacement cost less depreciation. Some jurisdictions use the broad evidence rule in determining ACV, a method by which all relevant facts—including depreciation and market value—may be used to determine actual cash value. (See Market Value)

A.M. Best is an information agency and publisher founded in 1899 to provide financial-strength and other information about insurance organizations.

Analytics is the branch of logic dealing with analysis. Business analytics is a term used for more sophisticated forms of business data analysis. Analytics closely resembles statistical analysis and data mining but tends to be based on physics modeling involving extensive computation. One new application of analytics is book of business analysis to maximize income while minimizing risk.

Assembly/assemblies refers to a group of building components. For example, a door assembly would include the basic door along with the door locks, handles, and hinges.

Cash flow underwriting is a business practice whereby insurers invested cash generated from premiums to offset underwriting losses. In the high interest rate environment of the late 1970s and early 1980s, these investment earnings, coupled with minimal or nonexistent underwriting profits, formed the basis of cash flow underwriting in property insurance.

Catastrophes From an insurance point of view, these are occurrences that affect significant numbers of insured risks in concentrated areas. These may be the result of nature (such as earthquakes, hailstorms, hurricanes) or man-made (such as arson or terrorism).

Class and Quality are subjective descriptors of home condition levels used within square-foot and unit-count methods; e.g. "class 1, 2 or 3" or "quality level 1, 2 or 3."

Coinsurance/co-insurance is the percentage by which an insured participates in a loss, or "co-insures" the loss, along with the insurance company. This is distinct from the deductible.

Combined ratio is the sum of the pure loss ratio and the underwriting expense ratio. The combined ratio combines the loss ratio and the expense ratio in order to provide a comparison between inflows and outflows from insurance operations.

Component-based estimating systems are software-based systems that use advanced computerization to incorporate the methodology of the detailed estimate once performed by the appraiser or loss-control professional. These programs assemble the component parts of the entire structure using simple descriptions of the property. These systems also take into account the interior of the property as well as exterior features and unique construction features, such as hillside construction.

Data Mining refers to examining databases to discover patterns in groups of data that can be used to predict future outcomes. For example, data mining valuation records can help insurance companies find customers with common home characteristics. True data mining actually discovers previously unknown relationships among the data, essentially deriving more meaningful data.

Depreciation is the lowering of value due to considerations such as age, deterioration, or functionality.

Drive-by inspection refers to the practice of inspecting a building to determine its value and condition without entering the building.

E.H. Boeckh is a company providing construction and building information to the insurance industry since 1930. Boeckh merged with Marshall & Swift to become Marshall & Swift / Boeckh, also known as MSB.

Endorsement is a written agreement attached to an insurance policy that amends the coverage by adding or subtracting coverage.

Estimated Market Value is the most probable price a willing buyer would pay for a specific home in a competitive market. It is important that the value of the land be deducted from the purchase price or *total market value* of the property in order to arrive at the home's estimated market value.

Exclusions are the parts of a policy that remove or restrict coverage. Common exclusions to most policies include war, intentional loss, governmental action, etc. Certain causes of loss, or perils, also may be excluded, such as in a property insurance policy in which the peril of flood is excluded.

Expert systems are computer programs that solve problems or perform tasks generally performed by human experts. An expert system follows a series of "Yes" and "No" questions or rules to mimic each step a human takes to make a decision. These computer programs use knowledge, facts, and reasoning techniques to solve problems and are part of a general category of computer applications known as *artificial intelligence.*

FAIR plans (Fair Access to Insurance Requirements) are state insurance plans that provide fire and extended coverage (in some states homeowners coverage) to insureds not qualifying for insurance through the voluntary market.

Five-digit ZIP code level or six-character Canadian postal code level refers to the first five digits in the U.S. Post Office ZIP+4 postal code system and to all six characters in the Canadian postal code. Research shows that home building costs can vary widely within the three-digit ZIP or postal code level, which is why modern valuation systems now research and provide labor and material costs at the five-digit ZIP or six-character Canadian postal code level.

Footprint is a name for the outline that the exterior of a residence or building would leave on a level site.

GI Bill or The Servicemen's Readjustment Act (1944) is a law designed to reduce the possibility of postwar depression brought on by widespread unemployment. In June 1943 the National Resources Planning Board recommended a series of programs for education and training. Signed into law in 1944 and often called "the GI Bill of Rights," it offered Federal aid to help veterans adjust to civilian life in the areas of hospitalization, purchase of homes and businesses, and, especially, education. By 1955, 4.3 million home loans had been granted, with a total face value of $33 billion. In addition, veterans were responsible for buying 20 percent of all new homes built after the war. (Source: An act to provide Federal Government aid for the readjustment in civilian life of returning World War II veterans, June 22,1944; Enrolled Acts and Resolutions of Congress, 1789-1996; General Records of the United States Government; Record Group 11, National Archives.)

GIS is the acronym for Geographic Information Systems. The utility of GIS is its ability to analyze the spatial information contained on maps. GIS uses the computer to process data related to space, in addition to words and numbers.

Guaranteed replacement cost policy or endorsement is a type of policy or endorsement that stipulates that, should a building need to be replaced due to an insured loss, the insurer will replace it with like kind and quality, without consideration for depreciation and regardless of the policy limit in force at the time of loss.

Hard costs include labor, material, and equipment-related building costs. These costs are typically higher in a reconstruction environment than in new construction due to such factors as economies of scale, less efficient scheduling, access problems, etc.

Hazard is a physical condition that increases the likelihood of a loss or the possible severity of a loss (e.g. smoking, improper storage of flammable materials, or proximity to a sink hole, brush fire zone, a coastal region, etc.)

High-value (mansion grade) homes are characterized by a sophisticated level of construction complexity. These homes are generally unique, architect-designed structures intended to make a statement about their owners. These homes are grand in scale and finish, with a number of characteristics (superstructure, substructure, elaborate roof lines and footprints, one or more wings, etc.) that clearly distinguish them from "McMansions." For a complete discussion of high-value homes, refer to Chapter 6 and Appendix 5.

High-worth area is an area characterized by higher economic conditions for the population, including greater personal wealth, upscale retail and service establishments, and a higher concentration of upscale and mansion-grade homes. The increased prices of goods and services in these areas, often a factor of what the market can bear, is a condition sometimes referred to as "The Hollywood Effect." The soft costs of construction and restoration, especially overhead and profit, are typically higher in high-worth areas than in neighboring non-high-worth areas.

Institute for Building and Home Safety (IBHS) is a nonprofit association involved in communication, education, engineering, and research about the causes of property losses. The institute's mission is to conduct research and advocate improved construction, maintenance, and preparation practices. Its members are insurers and reinsurers conducting business in the United States.

Indemnity (Principle of) is the concept that an insurer should restore the insured to his or her preloss condition.

Indexes are construction inflation factors that are used by insurance companies to trend the value of insured dwellings on a year-to-year basis instead of revaluing the dwellings annually. An index works by representing an average change in residential construction costs, weighted for segments of the country.

Insurance Services Office (ISO) is a company providing statistical and actuarial information as well as advisory policy forms and other services to the property and casualty insurance industry.

Insurance to value is the concept in property insurance of insuring a building for its full replacement value or reconstruction cost.

Insurable value is a quantified dollar amount that indicates insurance need and risk desirability of a particular structure.

Law of similar structures is a formula-based method for calculating coverage limits, which dictated that the home replacement cost was roughly equal to the prevailing square-foot cost for new construction in a designated geographic region.

Local/location multipliers are adjustment factors based on local labor and material costs used to localize base costs (as compared to national average costs).

Loss is the actual damage incurred under the coverage provisions of the insurance contract.

Market value is the probable price a property will sell for, with a knowledgeable buyer and seller acting prudently, for self-interest and not under undue duress. Market value is often erroneously used as a synonym for insurable value.

Marshall & Swift is a company providing construction and building information to the insurance industry since 1932. Marshall & Swift merged with E.H. Boeckh to become Marshall & Swift/Boeckh, also known as MSB.

McMansions are large, even oversized, *lavish-appearing* homes often built on speculation and usually built from standard plans that substitute size and volume for class and style. The plans often blend various motifs and elements of style that are not architecturally compatible with the neighborhood. Most McMansions utilize materials commonly used in homes that are more typical of what might be called main street neighborhoods. McMansions typically lack the premium-grade materials, unique designs, and careful craftsmanship found in a true high-value or mansion-grade home.

National Association of Insurance Commissioners (NAIC) Formed in 1871, the NAIC is a voluntary organization of the chief U.S. insurance regulatory officials of each of the fifty states, plus the District of Columbia and the five U.S. territories. Its objective is to help state insurance regulators protect consumers while helping to maintain the financial stability of the insurance industry.

National Underwriter Company is a publishing company that provides insurance and financial industry news, books, software, and other reference materials.

Outsourcing refers to the transfer of the operating responsibility for the performance of specific functions previously performed within a company's operations to an outside organization expert in those functions.

Overhead and Profit With respect to property, overhead and profit are components of the total cost of construction, remodeling, or reconstruction, which is comprised of materials, labor, equipment, overhead, and profit.

There are two kinds of **Overhead**: General Overhead and Job-Related Overhead. *General Overhead* relates to a broad variety of costs typically involved in doing business: office staff, office rent, office supplies, office equipment, utilities (telephones, electric, heat, etc.), sales, marketing and advertising costs, finance charges, etc. *Job-Related Overhead* refers to costs other than labor and material costs that are directly related to a specific project: building permits, fees and inspections, utility hook-up charges, construction drawings (blueprints), surveys, erosion control (silt fences, etc.), construction driveway, culvert or curb cut, interior cleaning of the building prior to occupancy, and site security.

Profit is a positive return on investment and in building construction, remodeling, or reconstruction, is the fee charged by a general contractor for construction services provided. It is related to the entrepreneurial risk that the contractor undertakes simply by being in the construction business.

Perils and Hazards are terms that are often used when discussing loss exposures. A peril is a cause of a loss (e.g. fire, burglary, collision, or flood). A hazard is anything that increases the likelihood of a loss or the possible severity of a loss (e.g. smoking, improper storage of flammable materials, proximity to a brush fire zone, etc.).

Plateline Studies are studies performed to analyze total losses. The name comes from building construction terms and refers to the bottom "plate" of a studded wall, which is attached to the foundation. If the entire structure is destroyed down to the foundation, it is said to be "lost to the plateline."

Premiums are those monies paid by the insured to an insurance company in exchange for insurance coverage.

Quantity Survey is a method used to estimate construction cost. The method is highly detailed and involves estimating the quantities needed for every building material, plus labor cost, based on the comprehensive interior and exterior details of the home.

Reconstruction Cost is the cost to construct, at current prices, an exact duplicate or replica of the building, using like kind and quality materials, construction standards, design, layout, and quality of workmanship. "Equal quality and utility" may be substituted where necessary for "like kind and quality." Reconstruction Cost, which is generally higher than Replacement Cost New, also includes site-specific and process-related costs and fees not included in Replacement Cost New valuations.

Replacement Cost/Replacement Cost New is the cost to replace an entire building with one of "equal quality and utility." Replacement costs are based on prices for labor, materials, overhead, profit, and fees that are in effect prior to the loss. Replacement costs assume that modern materials and current methods, designs, and layouts will be used to replace the building.

Reunderwriting/re-underwriting is the review of segments of or entire books of business.

Risk-specific valuation is the process of generating a replacement cost estimate through the identification of the actual components of a building.

Room count method is the same as unit-count method of estimating.

Segregated method is a method of valuing a structure developed by Marshall & Swift in which users price each major construction assembly individually to develop the total replacement cost of a building. This method involves identification of all the cost components of every assembly, based on quantities and types of materials found. Final estimates are a composite of all of the assemblies that make up the structure.

Soft costs are variable costs and generally include supervision, overhead, and profit. These costs are typically higher in a reconstruction or catastrophic environment than in new construction. Some of the less obvious soft costs include architect's fees and debris removal and disposal.

Square-foot valuation method is based upon the total square foot of the structure. It relied upon the *principle of similar structures*, which dictated that home replacement cost was roughly equal to the prevailing square-foot cost of new construction found anywhere in the nation. The square-foot or model-based method employs a set of base cost tables that are founded on prescribed or predetermined specifications and features. These specifications and features are reflective of a single base location and very specific characteristics. The costs were basically "cast in stone" when the product was initially released, with few if any changes made since that point in time.

Superstructure is an architecturally designed structural system within a large building engineered to withstand roof loads above and beyond those handled by framing methods common in smaller structures. Exceptionally large, high-value dwellings often employ an additional superstructure as well as columns and beams to support ceilings and roofs.

Three-digit ZIP code level refers to the first three digits in the five-digit U.S. Post Office ZIP code system and/or the first three characters of the six-character Canadian postal code. Research shows that home building costs can vary widely within the three-digit ZIP or postal code level, which is why modern valuation systems now research and provide labor and material costs at the five-digit ZIP or postal code level.

Total-component estimating system is a term coined by Marshall & Swift to describe its proprietary component-based valuation systems.

Tract housing refers to low-cost, mass-produced housing usually built by one developer on a large *tract* or expanse of land (subdivision) characterized by repetitive, simple designs. A classic case of this type of housing was Levittown, Long Island, which was the model on which many post-World War II suburban communities were based. The advent of homeowners insurance and the need for a simple valuation method can be traced to the emergence of tract housing.

Underinsurance/underinsured is the condition present whenever there is insufficient coverage on a structure to replace it at the time of loss.

Underwriting expense ratio is the percentage of premiums that goes to pay an insurer's operating expenses.

Unique construction refers to construction features that are uncommon and thus may be overlooked in the valuation of a property unless a detailed valuation system is used.

Unit-count method is also known as the room-count method. This approach is used exclusively on residential structures and involves counting the total number of construction units and rooms found in a dwelling and determining the valuation based on that count, adjusted for construction class and location.

Yuppie refers to a Young Urban Professional with a well-compensated professional job and an affluent lifestyle.

Appendix 1

Engineering Knowledge Tables

A well-designed component-based estimating system automatically accounts for local engineering conditions and requirements when determining replacement cost estimates. These requirements can vary widely from one geographical area to another. They include different construction assemblies for dealing with such items as heavy snow loads, heating and cooling requirements, frost depth, wind and fire conditions, and seismic activity.

The databases used by more sophisticated component-based estimating systems include various engineering knowledge tables to identify local building requirements. These tables are built using the intelligence of Geographic Information System (GIS) technologies, and, for each postal code, identify the appropriate zone for each of these building requirements. All the user has to do is enter a ZIP or Canadian postal code and the system should automatically build the house, construction assembly by construction assembly, to meet the current building requirements and building codes of the local area.

By comparison, the square-foot and unit-cost methods start with a cost for the standard, most common grade of house, roof, kitchen, etc., then attempt to adjust it by some average modifiers to try to account for local engineering conditions. However, given the geographic number of variations across North America, they frequently result in estimates that vary widely from the appropriate amount. The advanced technology of component-based estimating systems provides local, risk-specific cost information on individual homes. This significantly lowers the frequency of estimates that vary significantly from the correct reconstruction cost.

The following discussion summarizes the main engineering conditions and requirements that should be addressed by a sophisticated component-based valuation system. Each of these includes the geocoded map generated by a GIS system showing the division of areas of North America into various zones, each requiring different construction assemblies to meet local engineering requirements. These maps graphically illustrate the data contained in various engineering knowledge tables. They are followed by examples of how engineering requirements can differ due to local environmental conditions.

Seismic Zones

A Seismic Zone knowledge table divides the United States into several seismic zones based on the risk of earthquakes causing damage to structures (from minimal damage in Zones 1 and 2 to major damage in Zones 3 and 4). The shaking and ground upheaval associated with earthquakes can significantly damage or weaken a home's frame and can lift the entire home off its foundation. Because of this, homes in the seismic zones with a higher risk of damage need to have earthquake-resistant designs. The following figures illustrate some of the engineering considerations in seismic areas for a wood-frame house.

Anchoring the Frame to the Foundation

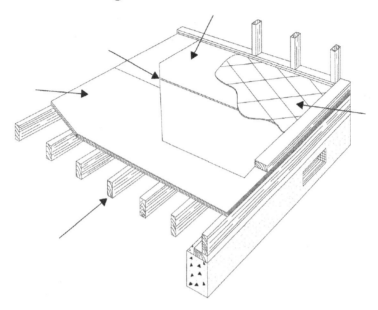

Without this anchoring, the house can move off its foundation. Typically, anchor bolts are installed every four to six feet to fasten the sill plate to the foundation.

Sheerwall Strengthening

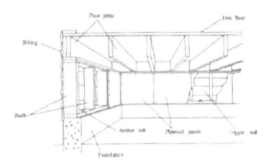

When an earthquake shakes a home from side to side, strong sheerwalls help the house resist this swaying. This is especially true of cripple walls, which are the wood stud walls in the crawl space between the top of the foundation and the first floor. If the cripple walls are not braced using plywood or diagonal bracing, the house can collapse. Typically, cripple walls are braced using plywood, with vent holes drilled to prevent moisture build-up and wood rotting.

Continuous Load Path

The use of a connection system to create a continuous load transfer path from the foundation to the rafters helps to strengthen the house and decrease the chances of damage from an earthquake. This includes using connectors to tie the entire structure of the house together, including connecting the frame studs to the sill plate, the studs on one floor to the studs on the next floor, and the roof rafters/trusses to the wall top plates.

Rooms over Garages

In many cases, the weight of a second-story room over a large garage door opening could cause it to collapse in an earthquake (depending on the relationship of the garage walls and door opening to the rest of the home). Typically, such openings are strengthened by bracing the area around the door with plywood or installing a steel frame.

Rooms over Garages

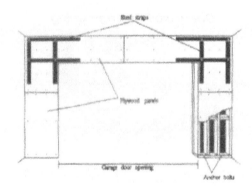

Although this list of examples is not exhaustive, it illustrates the engineering considerations for a wood-frame home in areas with high risk of earthquake damage. In a component-based system with a seismic knowledge table, the system will automatically assemble the costs associated with the need to bolt the frame to the foundation, brace the cripple wall with plywood, and tie and strengthen the garage door opening when there is a room above the garage.

Wind Conditions

WIND SPEED

Annual extreme values measured in mph at 30' above ground.

A Wind Speed knowledge table categorizes postal codes into one of several basic wind speed categories. In areas of higher wind speeds, houses need to have strengthened roof sheathing, roof cover, and sheerwalls, and need a connection system to create a continuous load transfer path from the foundation to the rafters. As in high-risk seismic zones, reinforcement is accomplished by connecting the frame studs to the sill plate, the studs on one floor to the studs on the next floor, and the roof rafters/trusses to the wall top plates.

Frost Penetration

ANNUAL AVERAGE FRONT PENETRATION

A Frost Penetration knowledge table divides a country into several zones based on the average annual depth of frost penetration. For homes that do not have basements, the foundation must be deep enough to be below the frost line to avoid freezing and cracking or movement generated by the expansion and contraction of the earth.

Advanced component-based valuation systems can use this type of knowledge table to set the foundation depth required in a postal code area for homes that do not have basements or appropriate insulation for shallow foundations. This includes calculating the cost for foundation excavation, forming, and concrete, etc., that are appropriate for the foundation depth required.

Insulation
INSULATION R-VALUES

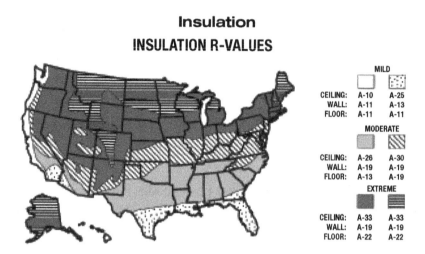

	MILD	
CEILING:	A-10	A-25
WALL:	A-11	A-13
FLOOR:	A-11	A-11
	MODERATE	
CEILING:	A-26	A-30
WALL:	A-19	A-19
FLOOR:	A-13	A-19
	EXTREME	
CEILING:	A-33	A-33
WALL:	A-19	A-19
FLOOR:	A-22	A-22

An Insulation knowledge table divides a country into several zones based on the insulation required in homes for floors, walls, and ceilings.

The table is used by a component-based valuation system to determine the R-rating required for the insulation in a given postal code area and, thus, the cost of the insulation. In certain cases, this affects the cost of the framing and/or exterior wall sheathing. For example, R-19 insulation for exterior walls can be obtained by combining 3-5/8" fiberglass batt insulation and 1" polystyrene sheathing or by using 6-1/2" fiberglass batt insulation. The latter requires framing greater than 2" x 4" (because the batt is 6-1/2" thick).

Heating & Cooling Days

ANNUAL AVERAGE TOTAL HEATING DEGREE DAYS

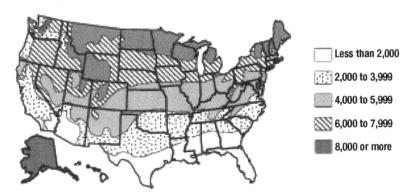

Less than 2,000
2,000 to 3,999
4,000 to 5,999
6,000 to 7,999
8,000 or more

ANNUAL AVERAGE TOTAL COOLING DEGREE DAYS

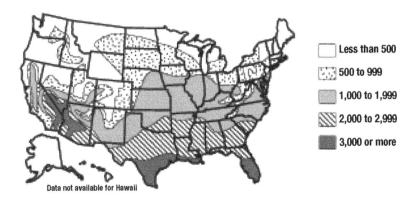

Less than 500
500 to 999
1,000 to 1,999
2,000 to 2,999
3,000 or more

Data not available for Hawaii

Heating degree days measure the need for heating. Each degree of a day's average temperature below 65° F is one heating degree day. For example, a day with an average temperature of 55° F has ten heating degrees days. Similarly, cooling degree days are a measure of the need for air conditioning. Each degree of a day's average temperature above 65° F is one cooling degree day. For example, a day with an average temperature of 80° F has fifteen cooling degree days.

A Heating and Cooling Degree Day knowledge tables divides a country into several zones based on heating and cooling degree days respectively. Component-based systems use these values, together with the size of the home, to determine the typical type and size of heating or cooling units needed for the home, and thus prices the appropriate unit to meet those requirements.

Snowfall

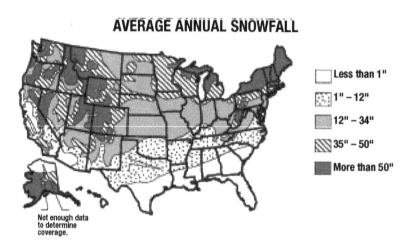

A Snowfall knowledge table divides a country into several zones based on average annual snowfall. In areas with heavier snowfall, component-based systems use the values in this table to increase the roof's slope and strengthen its structure to support the snow loads.

Appendix 2

Individual Home Characteristics

When *Insuring to Value* was first written in 1995, Marshall & Swift had performed over 500,000 detailed, risk-specific estimates on homes in the United States. Most of those estimates were archived in electronic database format, although many were still delivered in print. Each complete individual record contained information about six important home characteristics:

- Year Built

- Square Footage

- Style

- External Materials

- Internal Features

- ZIP or postal code

This process resulted in one of the most extensive databases in existence detailing individual home characteristics across the country. Two very significant conclusions were drawn from studying this database. First was that greater numbers and more detailed knowledge tables would be needed by model-based estimating systems to improve their reliability. However, the second conclusion was that the significant margin of error inherent in using any model-based system ruled out their effectiveness.

Accuracy Requires Detailed Knowledge Tables

By incorporating more knowledge tables or assumption sets of predominant home characteristics into any residential insuring-to-value estimating system, one can improve the reliability of the assumptions used in model-based estimating systems. These systems can utilize Geographical Information System methodologies to incorporate more localized home characteristic information. However, research showed that this action only *marginally* improves the accuracy of the broad-based modeling systems, which are based solely on generic assumption sets rather than on detailed, observable home characteristics.

Two following examples illustrate the limitations of relying heavily on geographical assumptions. Figure A2.1 illustrates the variation in the materials used for the exterior walls of homes in three different states, together with the national average of each of the same exterior wall materials.

Figure A2.1

Variation in Exterior Wall Materials				
Exterior Wall Type	**National Average**	**California**	**Florida**	**Pennsylvania**
Wood Siding	22.7%	31.2%	21.8%	17.5%
Aluminum/Vinyl Siding	28.0%	2.8%	5.1%	36.1%
Brick Veneer	12.5%	0.7%	7.5%	11.1%
Stucco on Frame	5.1%	55.9%	4.6%	2.2%
Solid Brick	13.8%	0.6%	4.2%	15.5%
Stucco on Masonry	7.2%	5.5%	42.7%	4.1%
Other	10.7%	3.3%	14.1%	13.5%

One can readily see in the first example that there are few norms in the frequency of use of exterior wall materials around the country. In this example, the two most predominant cases, stucco on frame in California and stucco on masonry in Florida, occur in about half of the cases. While knowledge such as this allows for far more localized assumption sets, *even these assumptions are incorrect in about 50 percent of the cases*. One can readily see that the frequency and magnitude of estimating error from this one aspect alone can vary widely. Fortunately, in this situation, a physical inspector, or possibly an agent, can readily obtain this information based on visual inspection and incorporate it into the estimate.

Figure A2.2 illustrates the variation in interior wall construction, which varies significantly by the year the home was built.

Figure A2.2

	Variation in Interior Wall Materials			
Wall Type	**Up to 1940**	**1941- 1950**	**1951- 1960**	**1960- Today**
Drywall	26.3%	44.5%	62.9%	91.1%
Plaster	69.5%	50.7%	33.6%	5.5%
Other	4.2%	4.8%	3.5%	3.4%

The second example is clearly more challenging. Here again, no single material is predominant in usage, and, again, the cost differences among the various materials will be of great significance to the overall estimate. Although there are clear variations in interior wall material used in different geographical areas, the relative frequency of such usage is more highly correlated with age of home and extent of subsequent remodeling.

The greater challenge, beyond creating more precise assumption sets, is to be able to specifically identify the actual building materials involved on a home-by-home basis. Physical inspectors and agents traditionally have been unable to gather this information for homes because they were unable to get into the home, the estimating systems they used did not allow them to incorporate this type of information, or they were simply not trained to identify and appreciate the importance of these, and similar, detailed characteristics. When one carries this thought to upgraded kitchens or baths (versus standard), interior wall finishes, etc., one can only imagine the randomness of accuracy of the resulting estimates.

Inherent Error in Model-based Methods

The second area of valuable information that came out of analyzing the extensive database of home characteristics was the inherent significance of the margin of error of using *any* model-based system for ITV determination. It was obvious that the cumulative effect of years of custom building, remodeling, and other individualized building activities had, in fact, resulted in the housing stock in North America being so dissimilar that modeling techniques were simply no longer reliable primary methods for estimating insurable values. Considerations such as geographically-based engineering requirements incorporating weather, seismic, or building code requirements were and still are generically reliable in their specific areas and properly should be incorporated into an appropriate estimating system. Beyond that, the database indicated that broad-based assumptions, even though they may be geographically or otherwise fine-tuned, essentially only lead to more sophisticated "guesstimating".

An example of the impact that making assumptions has on a replacement cost estimate can be displayed simply by considering the differences in cost between two homes that are identical, other than one having a stucco on frame exterior wall and drywall interior walls, while the other has wood siding and plaster interiors.

By using simplistic square foot techniques, which have been so prevalent in the insurance industry, it is likely that an inspector or agent would calculate an identical replacement cost for both of these residences. Typically, the square foot method asks the user to identify whether the building's exterior wall is frame, masonry, or veneer construction. However, the actual exterior wall type is not directly incorporated into the valuation. In addition, because the interior wall types are assumed as part of the "model" behind the square foot costs, it is virtually impossible to alter the estimate based on the actual interior wall construction materials.

However, using total component systems, these construction differences can be identified and used to calculate an appropriate replacement cost.

Figure A2.3

Wood Siding Exterior **Plaster Interiors**	
ABC Insurance 123 Hill Street Anywhere, USA 12345	
COST AS OF: 03/2006	TOTAL
FOUNDATIONS	$7,036
SLAB ON GRADE	3,058
FRAMING	16,249
ROOF COVER	4,454
EXTERIOR WALLS, DOORS, WINDOWS	18,890
INTERIOR WALLS, DOORS	23,799
WALL FINISHES	4,325
FLOORING	6,890
CEILINGS	11,135
EQUIPMENT	14,709
HEATING AND AIR CONDITIONING	4,611
PLUMBING	6,929
ELECTRICAL SYSTEMS	4,399
100% INSURABLE REPLACEMENT COST	$126,484

Figure A.2.4

Stucco on Frame Exterior **Drywall Interior**	
ABC INSURANCE 23 HILL STREET ANYWHERE, USA 12345	
COST AS OF: 03/2006	TOTAL
FOUNDATIONS	$ 7,036
SLAB ON GRADE	3,058
FRAMING	16,249
ROOF COVER	4,454
EXTERIOR WALLS, DOORS WINDOWS	14,462
INTERIOR WALLS, DOORS	15,628
WALL FINISHES	4,325
FLOORING	6,890
CEILINGS	3,790
EQUIPMENT	14,709
HEATING AND AIR CONDITIONING	4,611
PLUMBING	6,929
ELECTRICAL SYSTEMS	4,399
100% INSURABLE REPLACEMENT COST	$ 106,540

The impact is shown in Figures A2.3 and A2.4. As you can see, the estimate of the home with wood siding and plaster interiors has an insurable replacement cost of $126,484 while the home with stucco on frame and drywall interiors would cost $106,540 to replace. The $19,944 difference is quite substantial, especially because we only considered two characteristics in the make-up of the two homes.

By identifying the specific components of the home, the accuracy of the replacement cost estimate is greatly enhanced. The more assumptions that are drawn into the equation, the more likely the estimate will be in error.

Capturing the Most Salient Home Characteristics

Today, MSB has amassed an extensive database of estimates for over 8.1 million North American homes. Experience gained from reviewing these estimates and thousands of plate line (total loss) records reveals a need more even more information to properly value homes. Collecting at minimum the categories of information in the following outline ensures that the unique, individual characteristics of each home will be defined.

Minimum Home Characteristics

- 5-digit ZIP code (6-character in Canada)

- Foundation

- Number of families

- Exterior wall material

- Year built

- Roofing material

- Style

- Attached structures

- Number of stories

- Specialty features

- Total living area

- Kitchens and baths

- Heating and air conditioning

Utilizing the minimum thirteen categories of information to calculate replacement values for the homes would ensure premiums that are more properly aligned with risks, improving carrier profitability. In addition, using the information would positively impact policy retention and improve carriers' relationships with policyholders, consumer advocates, and insurance regulators.

Appendix 3

Catastrophes: The Insurance to Value Wildcard

The catastrophic events that concern insurers most today are remarkably similar to those they witnessed when the first edition of this book was written. There is, however, an important difference between then and now.

In 1989 and 1990, hurricanes were a wake-up call because the industry's drastic undervaluation problems were highlighted by carriers' unprofitable results. In contrast, 2005—the costliest year in history for the industry with total insured property losses estimated at $83 billion—was definitely *not* the worst year for insurer profitability: the combined ratio for the property and casualty industry was nearly break-even at 100.9, despite a reported $5 billion underwriting loss as of this writing. Many market factors contributed to this low combined ratio, not the least of which were increased premiums in the years immediately preceding 2005 that were supported by more accurate property valuation and assessment.

Figure A3.1

Hurricanes Making Landfall in North America in 2005	
Hurricane	**Date**
Hurricane Cindy	July 3-7
Hurricane Dennis	July 4-13
Hurricane Emily	July 11-21
Hurricane Irene	August 4-18
Hurricane Katrina	August 23-30
Hurricane Maria	September 1-10
Hurricane Nate	September 5-10
Hurricane Ophelia	September 6-17
Hurricane Philippe	September 17-23
Hurricane Rita	September 18-26
Hurricane Stan	October 8-11
Hurricane Vince	October 8-11
Hurricane Wilma	October 15-25
Hurricane Beta	October 26-31
Hurricane Epsilon	November 29-December 8

In 2005, North America saw the most active Atlantic tropical storm season ever, with twenty seven named storms and fifteen hurricanes including Katrina, the worst natural disaster in United States history. Hurricanes Katrina, Rita, and Wilma are estimated to cost the industry over $38 billion, $5 billion, and $9 billion, respectively, in insured property losses, with total property losses estimated at $83 billion. This is in stark contrast to storms prior to 2005, as illustrated in Figure A3.2. This table is derived from the National Hurricane Center's Tropical Cyclone Reports.

Figure A3.2

Hurricane Costs, 1990 – 2004			
Rank	**Hurricane**	**Year**	**Category**	**Damage**
1	Andrew (SE FL, SE LA)	1992	5	$ 43,672,000,000.00
2	Charley (SW FL)	2004	4	$ 15,000,000,000.00
3	Ivan (AL/NW FL)	2004	3	$ 14,200,000,000.00
4	Frances (FL)	2004	2	$ 8,900,000,000.00
5	Jeanne (FL)	2004	3	$ 6,900,000,000.00
6	Allison (N TX)	2001	(Tropical Storm)	$ 5,829,000,000.00
7	Floyd(Mid-Atlantic & NE U.S.)	1999	2	$ 5,764,000,000.00
8	Fran (NC)	1996	3	$ 4,525,000,000.00
9	Opal (NW FL, AL)	1995	3	$ 4,324,000,000.00
10	Isabel (Mid-Atlantic)	2003	2	$ 3,643,000,000.00
11	Bob (NC, NE U.S.)	1991	2	$ 2,593,000,000.00
12	Iniki (Kaua'i, HI)	1992	(Unknown)	$ 2,563,600,000.00
13	Georges (USVI, PR)	1998	3	$ 2,276,000,000.00
14	Marilyn (USVI, PR)	1995	2	$ 1,900,000,000.00

Source: NOAA (National Oceanic and Atmospheric Administration) Technical Memorandum NWS (National Weather Service) TPC-1.

Hurricanes have also far outstripped the costs of earthquakes, as shown in figure A3.3:

Figure A3.3

The Ten Most Costly U.S. Earthquakes ($millions)					
				Estimated property damage (1)	
Rank	Year	Location	Magnitude	Dollars when occurred	In 2005 dollars (2)
1	1994	Northridge, CA	6.7	$13-20,000	$17-26,000
2	1989	San Francisco Bay area; Loma Prieta, CA	6.9	$7,000	$11,025
3	1964	Alaska and west coast of United States (tsunami damage from earthquake near Anchorage, Alaska)	9.2	$ 500	$3,150
4	1971	San Fernando, CA	6.5	$ 553	$2,667
5	2001	Washington, Oregon	6.8	$2,305	$2,542
6	1987	Southern California; primarily in Los Angeles–Pasadena–Whittier area	5.9	$ 358	$ 615
7	1933	Long Beach, CA	6.3	$ 40	$ 601
8	1952	Kern County, CA	7.5	$ 60	$ 442
9	1992	Southern California; Landers–Joshua Tree–Big Bear	7.6	$ 92	$ 128
10	1992	Northern California Coast; Petrolia–Eureka	7.1	$ 66	$ 92

(1) Includes insured and uninsured losses.
(2) Adjusted to 2005 dollars by the Insurance Information Institute.

Source: Insurance Information Institute. Used with permission.

Impact on Reinsurers

Reinsurers did not enjoy the same good luck as their ceding clients. At the close of 2005, the Reinsurance Association of America estimated the reinsurance industry's loss ratio would reach 129 percent, up from 106.2 percent in 2004. That the combined ratio is now reported to be 144.8 percent is evidence that loss experience is increasing in the face of otherwise important improvements in the financial picture for primary markets. As a result, the reinsurance industry is expected to put pricing pressure on primary insurers going forward and to offer more favorable terms to those carriers that demonstrate a best-practices approach to insuring to value: using a total-component valuation approach, archiving data for risk-specific revaluation, communicating with policyholders to keep information current, and actively managing their books of business.

The Catastrophe Wildcard and Price Surge

As has long been the case, external events can disrupt the best-laid plans, as evidenced by fire and storm activity of 2003 to 2005. Following the 2005 hurricane season, meteorological experts predicted increased levels of hurricane activity projected to last through at least 2010. Changing weather patterns and expanded home construction in western states are expected to increase wildfire activity, and weather coupled with outdated and deteriorating infrastructure in northern states is predicted to bring increased flood damage. As a result, catastrophe-modeling company Risk Management Solutions announced in early 2006 that annualized insurance losses would increase by 40 percent on average across the Gulf Coast, Florida, and the Southeast, while FEMA predicts more flood-related damage in northern zones.

The fact that the catastrophes of 2005 did not produce the unprofitable operating results overall for primary insurers despite the $5 billion underwriting loss demonstrates that losses following catastrophes can be mitigated when insurers prepare for a future that is likely to bring such loss events. Insurers have been increasingly better prepared since their collective books of business were better managed in the years since 2000, when component-based estimating began to gain more widespread adoption in the property insurance industry.

Catastrophes present insurers and property owners with varied and significant problems that directly impact the insurance to value equation. These problems begin immediately after the disaster ends, when access to the affected area is limited and, as explained in Chapter 5, the laws of supply and demand impact both the scheduling and costs of adjusting losses and completing repairs.

In 2004, property reinsurers and the states of Florida and Mississippi requested a research initiative by MSB to add a demand surge component to the overall insurance to value equation. Research methods included interviews with local and national construction material suppliers, monitoring of shortages and material distribution and costs, contacting builders working in each area, performing on-the-ground research with claims adjusters and contractors, and reviewing claim files themselves. Because of the availability of data-archiving systems in the underwriting and claims arena, MSB was then able to combine this labor and material research with data on what had occurred in hundreds of thousands of active and closed claim files across wide segments of the Gulf states' economies, using the same technologies described earlier in this book. The research revealed cost variances, albeit not as draconian as reported by the press based on anecdotal information.

The final result was the MSB Price Surge Indicator™, an independently researched construction price-surge database for measuring the delta, or change, occurring in construction costs due to catastrophic events that had already occurred. (See Figure A3.4) The price surge database gives carriers information to immediately settle losses at fair prices reflective of actual local costs before irregularities set in. The database also provides information to

- measure, as often as monthly, the true local impact of price surges created by catastrophic events,

- isolate construction activity that falls out of the current norm, controlling prices and detecting fraud,

- follow the changes in extra-ordinary costs paid for losses locally at either the 5-digit ZIP code or smaller sub-segment of affected communities or states,

- understand true risk exposure based on proven pricing trends for improved book of business, modeling, and reinsurance management, and

- provide appropriate, independent research to add pricing endorsements or other enhanced pricing algorithms to property rating in order to price for catastrophic exposure going forward.

In addition to impacting the claims and underwriting process, surge indicator databases benefit both regulators and the general public, controlling costs and uncovering unscrupulous price gouging. Adding price surge data as an enhancement to a carrier's insurance-to-value program will also help actuaries assess the potential impact of catastrophic events on books of business.

Figure A3.4 Surge Pricing Impact

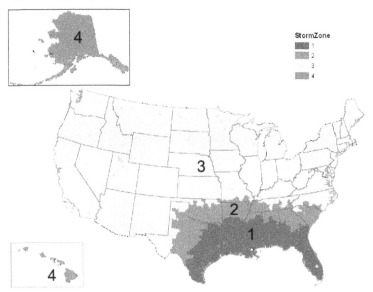

The map demonstrates the impact of price surge as cost variables changed following Hurricane Katrina. A Price Surge Indicator tracks the "ripple effect" as cost variables change across the affected area and spread actors the country.

Appendix 4

U.S. Homeowners Policies

The total number of homeowners policies in the United States by house year is 57,378,680.7, which is 83.5 percent of the total policies.

Source: 2003 Dwelling Fire, Homeowners Owner-Occupied, and Homeowners Tenant and Condominium /Cooperative Unit Owner's Insurance, published by the National Association of Insurance Commissioners. Reprinted with permission.

Appendix 5

Characteristics of High-Value Homes

A high-value home is much more than a big house with top-of-the-line finishes. MSB research conducted over the last seventy-five years reveals that a sophisticated level of construction complexity is predominant in these homes that, by definition, is not present in typical or what can be called main street homes, regardless of size. Of the nearly seventy-four million single-family dwellings in the United States, an estimated 8 percent of the housing market consists of high-value dwellings (United States Census Bureau, 2004 American Community Survey). In Canada's market of nearly seven million homes (Statistics Canada, 2003), an estimated 10 percent is considered to be high-value. Both markets have grown rapidly over the last few years, as favorable interest rates enabled entry into the high-value home market for greater numbers of homeowners.

Superstructure

Of the defining characteristics that separate true high-value homes from simply large-scale main street homes, the most important is superstructure. Most main street homes rely upon exterior and interior load-bearing walls to support roof loads, which will usually allow for clear spans of up to twenty feet. The open, expansive areas larger than 20′ x 20′ that are common features in high-value homes require additional superstructure for support.

To gain a few added feet of open space, horizontal framing members can be spaced closer together or doubled up, increasing framing costs by about 25 percent. But to obtain the dramatic spans incorporated into some high-value designs, builders rely on engineered framing components such as wood I-joists and open-web wood trusses, or they may employ structural systems more commonly found in commercial applications. An engineered approach to handling the roof load must be employed, and both the material components and the construction skill required are above and beyond the framing methods common in main street homes. This can double or triple the costs for floor or roof components alone, and costs are further increased if the designer must enlist the services of a licensed structural engineer.

Roof and Floors

The roof design and materials used in high-value homes also impact replacement cost to a greater degree than in a main street residence. High-value homes frequently have numerous gables, dormers, and decorative or ornamental features, creating intersecting valleys and ridge lines, multiple or compound roof pitches, and overhangs with varying widths. Most also have elaborate, nonrectangular footprints, further presenting roof design challenges and construction complexity.

Foundation and Support

Also associated with greater spans are the increased loads on the foundation imposed by the roof or floor framing members. Load transfer in high-value homes frequently produces significant loads concentrated on one or several points, requiring additional footings and foundations. Additionally, high-value residences built in extreme terrain present additional structural challenges. For example, building on a shoreline may require that the home be elevated on stilts or piers. Yet even the foundation for a home built on a slab can be deceptively complex in a high-value home. A one-story residence might be built with sections of the home at different levels and will not at all look like a ranch home. The slab may undulate to follow the natural contours of the site or as a design element to isolate a wing from the main section of the home.

Interior

Construction complexities in a high-value home affect the interior as well. Unlike a McMansion, where the grandeur may be superficial, a true high-value residence is functionally customized to the lifestyle of the homeowner and nearly always has numerous specialty rooms designed, equipped, and decorated with an explicit purpose in mind. For example, while a main street home or McMansion might have an exercise room, a high-value home might have a personal gymnasium better equipped than a health club. The layout and design of each specialty room in a high-value home involves the advice and expertise of specialized design and construction professionals charged with accommodating the exact needs of the homeowner.

Finally, a high-value home often has ceiling heights beyond that of a main street home. When ceiling heights reach ten feet and beyond, the overall proportions in each room become an important issue: as doors and windows get taller, they must also get wider to retain pleasing, harmonious proportions. This, of course, impacts reconstruction cost.

The number and significance of features that clearly differentiate high-value homes from typical main street homes, especially those that relate to superstructure and substructure, began to raise the question of the adequacy of relying on the same cost calculation assumptions used for main street homes to calculate replacement or reconstruction costs for high-value homes. In answering this question, MSB obtained detailed information about large numbers of single-family high-value homes, including blueprints, builders' costs, structural details, material details, additional features, and individual building characteristics, ultimately developing valuation methodologies and applications that reflected the differences between main street and high-value homes.

These differences are clearly illustrated in the following example of an actual 1.5-story, 4,100 square-foot home located in the Midwest. The home was first valued by using all data entry options typical for main street homes. It then was valued using the broader datasets and specialized knowledge tables that accommodated the sophisticated level of construction complexity in the sample home and enabled additional data entry options to capture the unique characteristics of the home.

This valuation exercise showed a wide variety of pertinent home features where cost variances per building system category were deficient by a range of from 10 percent to 300 percent. It also found an actual variance in the total value of the home of 206 percent, a cost differential that cannot be ignored when determining policy limits and premiums. This finding is especially important when considering the potential negative impact on the profitability of an entire book of business.

INDEX